SCHOLASTIC
News
Leveled Informational Texts

GRADE

M000239854

New York • Toronto • London • Auckland • Sydney
Mexico City • New Delhi • Hong Kong • Buenos Aires

Photos ©: cover top left: Westend61/Getty Images; cover center left: Mike Parry/Minden Pictures; cover center right: NHPA/Superstock, Inc.; cover bottom left: unkas_photo/iStockphoto; cover bottom right: Kenneth Garrett/Getty Images; 3 top and throughout: Courtesy Jane Goodall's Wild Chimpanzees/MacGillivray Freeman Films; 3 bottom: Kerryn Parkinson/Zuma Press; 12 and throughout: Reinhard Dirscherl/Getty Images; 13 and throughout: ake petchson/Shutterstock; 14 and throughout: Georgette Douwma/Getty Images; 22 and throughout: Renato Chalu/AP Images; 27 and throughout: Rod Veal/Zuma Press; 28 and throughout: Courtesy of United States Air Force; 37 and throughout: unkas_photo/iStockphoto; 38 and throughout: Ahmed Areef/EyeEm/Getty Images; 45 and throughout: Ruth Petzold/Getty Images; 46 and throughout: David McNew/Getty Images; 48 and throughout: Willyam Bradberry/Shutterstock; 57 and throughout: Stefan Rousseau/AP Images; 59 and throughout: Kenneth Garrett/Getty Images; 66 and throughout: Dawie Jacobs Photography/Shutterstock; 67 top and throughout: Meet Poddar/Shutterstock; 67 center and throughout: Rich Carey/Shutterstock; 67 bottom and throughout: Kerryn Parkinson/Zuma Press; 69 and throughout: Spumador/Shutterstock. Map by Jim McMahon, Scholastic Inc.

Editor: Maria L. Chang
Cover design by Michelle H. Kim
Interior design by Kay Petronio

Scholastic Inc., 557 Broadway, New York, NY 10012
ISBN: 978-1-338-28475-1
Copyright © 2019 by Scholastic Inc.
All rights reserved.
Printed in the U.S.A.
First printing, January 2019.

1 2 3 4 5 6 7 8 9 10   40   25 24 23 22 21 20 19

Table of Contents

Introduction

Finding quality informational texts at the appropriate level can be quite challenging. That's why we created this collection of compelling articles, which were originally printed in our award-winning classroom magazine *Scholastic News*. The passages have been carefully selected to engage students' interest and have been leveled to meet the needs of all readers. Each article comes in three Lexile levels. But because all versions of an article look alike, students need not know they're getting different levels. To identify the reading levels, simply look at the shape around the page numbers.

One way to build students' comprehension is to encourage them to mark up the text as they read—circling, underlining, or highlighting main ideas, supporting details, and key vocabulary words. This simple action helps them process what they're reading, making it easier to focus on important ideas and make connections. For more test-taking tips, photocopy and distribute the helpful hints below for students.

TEST-TAKING TIPS FOR STUDENTS:

- Make sure you understand each question fully before you answer it. Underline key words. Restate the question in your own words.

- Always refer to the text to find answers. It's a good idea to go back and reread parts of the text to answer a question.

- When you finish, check all your answers. You may find a mistake that you can correct.

- Most important, relax! Some people get nervous before a test. That's normal. Just do your best.

A Champion for Chimps

Jane Goodall may be human. But some chimpanzees think of her as family. That's because she lived with them for three decades. Goodall was the first person to study these apes in the wild. Her discoveries changed the way we see our closest animal relatives.

Goodall now works to protect these endangered primates and their habitats. She spoke to *Scholastic News* about her work.

Why did you decide to study chimpanzees?

Goodall: Growing up in England, I fell in love with Africa after reading the book *Tarzan of the Apes.* I dreamed of one day going there and living among the animals and writing books about them. It wasn't until I met the famous scientist Louis Leakey, in 1957, that I set out to study chimpanzees, at the age of 26. Leakey sent me to Africa to **observe** chimpanzees in the wild so we could learn more about how they behave.

What did you discover about them?

Goodall: One day in November 1960, something amazing happened. I came across my favorite chimpanzee, David Greybeard. He was stripping the leaves off a stalk of grass and pushing it into a termite mound. When he pulled out the stalk, it was covered with termites. He then began to eat them off the stalk. He had made a tool to fish the termites out of their mound! Until that time, people thought only humans made and used tools.

Over time, I also learned that chimpanzees hunt for and eat meat. Before that, people thought they were vegetarians. I also found that chimpanzees have long-lasting family bonds, much like we do.

What are the biggest threats to chimps?

Goodall: Chimpanzees are disappearing fast because their forest home in Africa is being destroyed. Without forests, chimpanzees will perish, and so will countless other animal and plant species.

In central Africa, chimpanzees are also disappearing because of the commercial hunting of wild animals for food. Sometimes chimpanzee mothers are killed for food, and the hunters take their babies to sell them to be used for entertainment or as pets.

Should people be allowed to have chimps as pets?

Goodall: No. Chimpanzees are wild animals that should stay in the forests of Africa. Sometimes people see chimpanzees in commercials and think they are cute and would make good pets. Nothing is further from the truth. The chimps in most commercials were likely taken from their mothers, and the training they endure can be cruel. And when they grow up, they become very strong and can be dangerous.

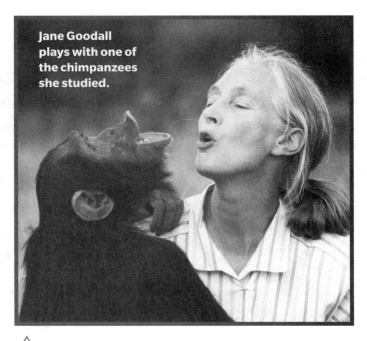

Jane Goodall plays with one of the chimpanzees she studied.

Name: _____

Directions: Read the article "A Champion for Chimps." Then answer the questions below.

1. Why did Goodall choose to include details about David Greybeard eating termites from a stalk?

   A. To introduce readers to her favorite chimp

   B. To illustrate how she discovered that chimps form family bonds

   C. To illustrate how she discovered that chimps use tools

   D. To prove that chimps make good pets

2. Explain how Goodall became interested in studying chimpanzees.

   _____

   _____

   _____

3. Read this sentence from the article and answer the question that follows.

   Leakey sent me to Africa to **observe** chimpanzees in the wild so we could learn more about how they behave.

   How would you define the word *observe* **as it's used in the text?**

   _____

   _____

4. Using at least two details from the text, explain how humans affect chimpanzees.

   _____

   _____

   _____

   _____

5. According to Goodall, how are chimpanzees like humans?

   _____

   _____

   _____

A Champion for Chimps

Jane Goodall may be human, but some chimpanzees think of her as family. That's because she lived with them for three decades. Goodall began studying chimps in 1960, in what is now Gombe National Park in Tanzania, a country on the east coast of Africa. Goodall was the first person to study these apes in the wild. Her discoveries changed the way we see our closest animal relatives.

Goodall now works to protect these endangered primates and their forest homes through the Jane Goodall Institute. She spoke to *Scholastic News* about her work and the importance of protecting chimps.

Why did you decide to study chimpanzees?

Goodall: Growing up in England, I fell in love with Africa after reading the book *Tarzan of the Apes*. I dreamed of one day going there and living among the animals and writing books about them. It wasn't until I met the famous scientist Louis Leakey, in 1957, that I set out to study chimpanzees, at the age of 26. Leakey sent me to Africa to **observe** chimpanzees in the wild so we could learn more about how they behave.

What did you discover about them?

Goodall: One day in November 1960, something amazing happened. I came across my favorite chimpanzee, David Greybeard. He was stripping the leaves off a stalk of grass and pushing it into a termite mound. When he pulled out the stalk, it was covered with termites. He then began to eat them off the stalk. He had made a tool to fish the termites out of their mound! Until that time, people thought only humans made and used tools.

Over time, I also learned that chimpanzees hunt for and eat meat. Before that, people thought they were vegetarians. I also found that chimpanzees have long-lasting family bonds, much like we do.

What are the biggest threats to chimps?

Goodall: Chimpanzees are disappearing fast because their forest home in Africa is being destroyed. Without forests, chimpanzees will perish, and so will countless other animal and plant species.

In central Africa, chimpanzees are also disappearing because of the commercial hunting of wild animals for food. Sometimes chimpanzee mothers are killed for food, and the hunters take their babies to sell them to be used for entertainment or as pets.

Should people be allowed to have chimps as pets?

Goodall: No. Chimpanzees are wild animals that should stay in the forests of Africa. Sometimes people see chimpanzees in commercials and think they are cute and would make good pets. Nothing is further from the truth. The chimps in most commercials were likely taken from their mothers, and the training they endure can be cruel. And when they grow up, they become very strong and can be dangerous.

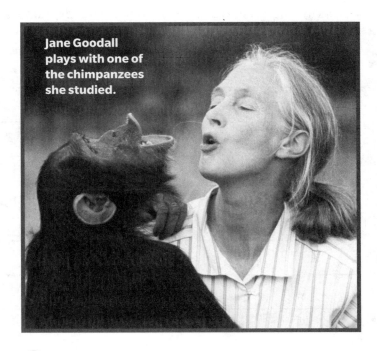

Jane Goodall plays with one of the chimpanzees she studied.

Scholastic News Leveled Informational Texts (Grade 5) © Scholastic Inc.

Name: _____

Directions: Read the article "A Champion for Chimps." Then answer the questions below.

1. **Why did Goodall choose to include details about David Greybeard eating termites from a stalk?**

    A. To prove that chimps make good pets

    B. To illustrate how she discovered that chimps use tools

    C. To introduce readers to her favorite chimp

    D. To illustrate how she discovered that chimps form family bonds

2. **Explain how Goodall became interested in studying chimpanzees.**

_____

_____

_____

3. **Read this sentence from the article and answer the question that follows.**

    Leakey sent me to Africa to **observe** chimpanzees in the wild so we could learn more about how they behave.

    How would you define the word *observe* as it's used in the text?

_____

_____

4. **According to Goodall, how are chimpanzees like humans?**

_____

_____

_____

_____

5. **Using at least two details from the text, explain how humans affect chimpanzees.**

_____

_____

_____

A Champion for Chimps

Jane Goodall may be human, but some chimpanzees think of her as family. That's because she lived with them for three decades. Goodall began studying chimps in 1960, in what is now Gombe National Park in Tanzania, a country on the east coast of Africa. As the first person to study these apes in the wild, Goodall made discoveries that changed the way we see our closest animal relatives.

Goodall now works to protect these endangered primates and their forest homes through the Jane Goodall Institute. The Institute also offers programs to help impoverished people who live near chimp habitats. Once people's own lives improve, the Institute hopes they will then take better care of their environment and the creatures in it.

Goodall spoke to *Scholastic News* about her work and the importance of protecting chimps.

Why did you decide to study chimpanzees?

Goodall: Growing up in England, I fell in love with Africa after reading the book *Tarzan of the Apes.* I dreamed of one day going there and living among the animals and writing books about them. It wasn't until I met the famous scientist Louis Leakey, in 1957, that I set out to study chimpanzees, at the age of 26. Leakey sent me to Africa to **observe** chimpanzees in the wild so we could learn more about how they behave.

What did you discover about them?

Goodall: One day in November 1960, something amazing happened. I came across my favorite chimpanzee, David Greybeard. He was stripping the leaves off a stalk of grass and pushing it into a termite mound. When he pulled out the stalk, it was covered with termites. He then began to eat them off the stalk. He had made a tool to fish the termites out of their mound! Until that time, people thought only humans made and used tools.

Over time, I also learned that chimpanzees hunt for and eat meat. Before that, people thought they were vegetarians. I also found that chimpanzees have long-lasting family bonds, much like we do.

What are the biggest threats to chimpanzees?

Goodall: Chimpanzees are disappearing fast because their forest home in Africa is being destroyed. Without forests, chimpanzees will perish, and so will countless other animal and plant species.

In central Africa, chimpanzees are also disappearing because of the commercial hunting of wild animals for food. Sometimes chimpanzee mothers are killed for food, and the hunters take their babies to sell them to be used for entertainment or as pets.

Should people be allowed to have chimps as pets?

Goodall: No. Chimpanzees are wild animals that should stay in the forests of Africa. Sometimes people see chimpanzees in commercials and think they are cute and would make good pets. Nothing is further from the truth. The chimps in most commercials were likely taken from their mothers, and the training they endure can be cruel. And when they grow up, they become very strong and can be dangerous.

Jane Goodall plays with one of the chimpanzees she studied.

Name: _____

Directions: Read the article "A Champion for Chimps." Then answer the questions below.

1. Explain how Goodall became interested in studying chimpanzees.

_____

_____

_____

2. Read this sentence from the article and answer the question that follows.

> Leakey sent me to Africa to **observe** chimpanzees in the wild so we could learn more about how they behave.

How would you define the word _observe_ as it's used in the text?

_____

_____

3. Why did Goodall choose to include details about David Greybeard eating termites from a stalk?

  A. To illustrate how she discovered that chimps form family bonds

  B. To introduce readers to her favorite chimp

  C. To prove that chimps make good pets

  D. To illustrate how she discovered that chimps use tools

4. Using at least two details from the text, explain how humans affect chimpanzees.

_____

_____

_____

_____

5. According to Goodall, how are chimpanzees like humans?

_____

_____

_____

If You Can't Beat 'Em, Eat 'Em!

1   Brightly colored stripes and long, feathery fins make lionfish look right at home in Florida's coral reefs. But these flashy fish are actually far from their natural habitat. And they're causing big trouble. Now, wildlife officials in Florida are asking people to strike back. How? By taking a knife and fork to the problem.

Fish Invasion

2   Lionfish are an invasive species in the United States. That term describes any animal or plant that is brought to a new habitat and harms native animals or plants.

3   Lionfish come from the Indian and western Pacific oceans. They were first spotted in U.S. waters off the Atlantic coast of Florida in the 1980s. They were probably aquarium pets that had been released into the wild.

4   Lionfish have no natural predators in these waters. So they quickly multiplied. Now they're found along much of the East Coast of the U.S. They've also been spotted in the Caribbean Sea and the Gulf of Mexico.

5   These invaders are disrupting the ecosystem around Florida's fragile coral reefs. Lionfish may look pretty. But they are ferocious predators. They eat just about every small fish in sight. And their big appetites mean trouble for more than just the fish they eat. Native predator fish, such as groupers, are left starving.

Stick a Fork in It?

6   Government agencies that protect fish and wildlife haven't had much luck in stopping the spread of lionfish. So they've turned to the public for help. Ad campaigns in Florida are promoting lionfish as a tasty dinner option.

7   Lionfish are already on the menu at several restaurants in Florida. Cooks have to take special care to prepare them. Their long fins are filled with venom that can sting your skin.

8   Florida is also encouraging fishermen to get in on the act. Residents usually need a special license to fish. But the state makes an exception for people who catch lionfish. Government officials hope these efforts will slow down the exploding number of lionfish.

9   "The likelihood of getting rid of every lionfish is pretty slim," explains Amanda Nalley. She is a fish and wildlife official in Florida. "What we're really looking to do is control the population."

10   Nalley and other experts say people may be the best hope for restoring balance to Florida's marine ecosystems. After all, we are the world's top predator.

Lionfish among corals

Name: _____

Directions: Read the article "If You Can't Beat 'Em, Eat 'Em!" Then answer the questions below.

1. **Which of the following statements best explains why lionfish have thrived in Florida's waters?**

   A. Now, wildlife officials in Florida are asking people to strike back. *(paragraph 1)*

   B. They were probably aquarium pets that had been released into the wild. *(paragraph 3)*

   C. Lionfish have no natural predators in these waters. *(paragraph 4)*

   D. They eat just about every small fish in sight. *(paragraph 5)*

2. **What is one effect that lionfish are having on the ecosystem in Florida's coral reefs?**

   A. Native predator fish are eating many lionfish.

   B. The populations of native fish are quickly increasing.

   C. Fishermen are no longer able to catch groupers.

   D. Groupers and other native predator fish have much less to eat.

3. **According to the article, what is one solution that Florida has come up with to address the lionfish problem?**

   A. Allowing residents to fish for lionfish without a license

   B. Introducing new kinds of fish to Florida's coral reefs

   C. Requiring restaurants to add lionfish to their menus

   D. Running ad campaigns promoting groupers as a good meal choice

4. **Which of the following can be concluded from the article?**

   A. It is probably not possible to completely remove lionfish from Florida's waters.

   B. Eating lionfish is the only way to control the invasive lionfish population.

   C. Fishing in Florida's waters is disrupting its marine ecosystems.

   D. Wildlife officials think that lionfish fit in well in Florida's coral reefs.

Name: _____

5. **Which sentence from the article best supports the answer to question 4?**

   A. Brightly colored stripes and long, feathery fins make lionfish look right at home in Florida's coral reefs. *(paragraph 1)*

   B. These invaders are disrupting the ecosystem around Florida's fragile coral reefs. *(paragraph 5)*

   C. Ad campaigns in Florida are promoting lionfish as a tasty dinner option. *(paragraph 6)*

   D. "The likelihood of getting rid of every lionfish is pretty slim," explains Amanda Nalley. *(paragraph 9)*

6. **The article ends by stating that experts think that the solution to the lionfish problem lies with people, the world's top predator. What do the experts mean? Why do you think the author ended the article with this point? Use details from the article to support your answer.**

_____

_____

_____

_____

_____

If You Can't Beat 'Em, Eat 'Em!

1   Brightly colored stripes and long, feathery fins make lionfish look right at home gliding around Florida's coral reefs. But these flashy fish are actually far from their natural habitat. And they're causing big trouble. Now, wildlife officials in Florida are asking people to strike back. How? By taking a knife and fork to the problem.

Fish Invasion

2   Lionfish are an invasive species in the United States. That term is used to describe any animal or plant that is brought to a new habitat and harms native animals or plants.

3   Lionfish are native to the Indian and western Pacific oceans. They were first spotted in U.S. waters off the Atlantic coast of Florida in the 1980s. They may have been aquarium pets that were released into the wild.

4   With no natural predators in these waters, the lionfish quickly multiplied. They're now found along much of the East Coast of the United States. They've also been spotted in the Caribbean Sea and the Gulf of Mexico.

5   These invaders are disrupting the ecosystem around Florida's fragile coral reefs. Lionfish may look pretty. But they are ferocious predators that eat just about every small fish in sight. And their big appetites mean trouble for more than just the fish they eat. The lack of food is starving out native predator fish, such as groupers.

Stick a Fork in It?

6   Government agencies that protect fish and wildlife haven't had much luck in stopping the spread of lionfish. So they've turned to the public for help. Ad campaigns in Florida are promoting lionfish as a tasty dinner option.

7   Lionfish are already on the menu at several restaurants in Florida. Cooks have to take special care to prepare them. Their long fins are filled with venom that can sting your skin.

8   Florida is also encouraging fishermen to get in on the act. Residents usually need a special license to fish. But the state recently made an exception for people who catch lionfish. Government officials hope these efforts will take a bite out of the exploding number of lionfish.

9   "The likelihood of getting rid of every lionfish is pretty slim," explains Amanda Nalley, a fish and wildlife official in Florida. "What we're really looking to do is control the population."

10   Nalley and other experts say people—the world's top predator—may be the best hope for restoring balance to Florida's marine ecosystems.

Lionfish among corals

Name: _____

Directions: Read the article "If You Can't Beat 'Em, Eat 'Em!" Then answer the questions below.

1. **Which of the following statements best explains why lionfish have thrived in Florida's waters?**

   A. But they are ferocious predators that eat just about every small fish in sight. *(paragraph 5)*

   B. With no natural predators in these waters, the lionfish quickly multiplied. *(paragraph 4)*

   C. They may have been aquarium pets that were released into the wild. *(paragraph 3)*

   D. Now, wildlife officials in Florida are asking people to strike back. *(paragraph 1)*

2. **What is one effect that lionfish are having on the ecosystem in Florida's coral reefs?**

   A. The populations of native fish are quickly increasing.

   B. Fishermen are no longer able to catch groupers.

   C. Groupers and other native predator fish have much less to eat.

   D. Native predator fish are eating many lionfish.

3. **According to the article, what is one solution that Florida has come up with to address the lionfish problem?**

   A. Introducing new kinds of fish to Florida's coral reefs

   B. Requiring restaurants to add lionfish to their menus

   C. Running ad campaigns promoting groupers as a good meal choice

   D. Allowing residents to fish for lionfish without a license

4. **Which of the following can be concluded from the article?**

   A. Eating lionfish is the only way to control the invasive lionfish population.

   B. It is probably not possible to completely remove lionfish from Florida's waters.

   C. Wildlife officials think that lionfish fit in well in Florida's coral reefs.

   D. Fishing in Florida's waters is disrupting its marine ecosystems.

5. **Which sentence from the article best supports the answer to question 4?**

   A. "The likelihood of getting rid of every lionfish is pretty slim," explains Amanda Nalley, a fish and wildlife official in Florida. *(paragraph 9)*

   B. Brightly colored stripes and long, feathery fins make lionfish look right at home gliding around Florida's coral reefs. *(paragraph 1)*

   C. These invaders are disrupting the ecosystem around Florida's fragile coral reefs. *(paragraph 5)*

   D. Ad campaigns in Florida are promoting lionfish as a tasty dinner option. *(paragraph 6)*

6. **The article ends by stating that experts think that the solution to the lionfish problem lies with humans, the world's top predator. What do the experts mean? Why do you think the author ended the article with this point? Use details from the article to support your answer.**

   _____

   _____

   _____

   _____

   _____

If You Can't Beat 'Em, Eat 'Em!

1   With their brightly colored stripes and long, feathery fins, lionfish look right at home gliding around Florida's coral reefs. But these flashy fish are actually far from their natural habitat—and they're causing big trouble. Wildlife officials in Florida are asking people to strike back by taking a knife and fork to the problem.

Fish Invasion

2   Lionfish are an invasive species in the United States. That term is used to describe any animal or plant that is brought to a new habitat and harms native animals or plants.

3   Lionfish are native to the Indian and western Pacific oceans. They were first spotted in U.S. waters off the Atlantic coast of Florida in the 1980s. They may have been aquarium pets that were released into the wild.

4   With no natural predators in these waters, the lionfish quickly multiplied. They're now found along much of the East Coast of the U.S. They've also been spotted in the Caribbean Sea and the Gulf of Mexico.

5   These invaders are disrupting the ecosystem around Florida's fragile coral reefs. Lionfish may look pretty, but they are ferocious predators that eat just about every small fish in sight. And their big appetites mean trouble for more than just the fish they eat. The lack of food is starving out native predator fish, such as groupers.

Stick a Fork in It?

6   Government agencies that protect fish and wildlife haven't had much luck in stopping the spread of lionfish. So they've turned to the public for help. Ad campaigns in Florida are promoting lionfish as a tasty dinner option.

7   Lionfish are already on the menu at several restaurants in Florida. Cooks have to take special care to prepare them. Their long fins are filled with venom that can sting your skin.

8   Florida is also encouraging fishermen to get in on the act. Residents usually need a special license to fish, but the state recently made an exception for people who catch lionfish. Government officials hope these efforts will take a bite out of the exploding number of lionfish.

9   "The likelihood of getting rid of every lionfish is pretty slim," explains Amanda Nalley, a fish and wildlife official in Florida. "What we're really looking to do is control the population."

10   Nalley and other experts say people—the world's top predator—may be the best hope for restoring balance to Florida's marine ecosystems.

Lionfish among corals

Scholastic News Leveled Informational Texts (Grade 5) © Scholastic Inc.

Name: _____

Directions: Read the article "If You Can't Beat 'Em, Eat 'Em!" Then answer the questions below.

1. **Which of the following statements best explains why lionfish have thrived in Florida's waters?**

   A. Wildlife officials in Florida are asking people to strike back by taking a knife and fork to the problem. *(paragraph 1)*

   B. Lionfish may look pretty, but they are ferocious predators that eat just about every small fish in sight. *(paragraph 5)*

   C. They may have been aquarium pets that were released into the wild. *(paragraph 3)*

   D. With no natural predators in these waters, the lionfish quickly multiplied. *(paragraph 4)*

2. **What is one effect that lionfish are having on the ecosystem in Florida's coral reefs?**

   A. Groupers and other native predator fish have much less to eat.

   B. Fishermen are no longer able to catch groupers.

   C. Native predator fish are eating many lionfish.

   D. The populations of native fish are quickly increasing.

3. **According to the article, what is one solution that Florida has come up with to address the lionfish problem?**

   A. Requiring restaurants to add lionfish to their menus

   B. Allowing residents to fish for lionfish without a license

   C. Running ad campaigns promoting groupers as a good meal choice

   D. Introducing new kinds of fish to Florida's coral reefs

4. **Which of the following can be concluded from the article?**

   A. Eating lionfish is the only way to control the invasive lionfish population.

   B. Wildlife officials think that lionfish fit in well in Florida's coral reefs.

   C. Fishing in Florida's waters is disrupting its marine ecosystems.

   D. It is probably not possible to completely remove lionfish from Florida's waters.

5. **Which sentence from the article best supports the answer to question 4?**

    A. These invaders are disrupting the ecosystem around Florida's fragile coral reefs. *(paragraph 5)*

    B. Ad campaigns in Florida are promoting lionfish as a tasty dinner option. *(paragraph 6)*

    C. "The likelihood of getting rid of every lionfish is pretty slim," explains Amanda Nalley, a fish and wildlife official in Florida. *(paragraph 9)*

    D. With their brightly colored stripes and long, feathery fins, lionfish look right at home gliding around Florida's coral reefs. *(paragraph 1)*

6. **The article ends by stating that experts think that the solution to the lionfish problem lies with humans, the world's top predator. What do the experts mean? Why do you think the author ended the article with this point? Use details from the article to support your answer.**

_____

_____

_____

_____

_____

Scholastic News Leveled Informational Texts (Grade 5) © Scholastic Inc.

Walking the Amazon

1   Imagine encountering 20-foot-long snakes and caiman crocodiles. Then imagine constantly worrying about drowning. That is exactly what happened to Ed Stafford. He went on a 2½-year journey along the Amazon River in South America.

2   In August 2010, Stafford became the first person to trek the entire length of the Amazon River. Stafford is from England. He wanted to do something that had never been done before. And he wanted to see the problems facing the Amazon region firsthand.

From Source to Sea

3   On April 2, 2008, Stafford began his journey at the source of the Amazon River, in Peru. From there, the river travels 4,200 miles eastward. It empties into the Atlantic Ocean in Maruda, Brazil. In August 2008, a guide, Gadiel "Cho" Sánchez Rivera, joined Stafford. On August 9, 2010, Stafford jumped into the ocean with Cho to celebrate finally reaching the end. Stafford had walked for 859 days.

4   It was a well-deserved celebration. Along the way, Stafford wore out several pairs of shoes. But that was the least of his problems. He braved stings from hundreds of wasps and bites from thousands of mosquitoes. He waded in water filled with electric eels and dodged snakes and scorpions. He also faced starvation.

5   That's not all. The chief of a native tribe in Peru said he'd kill Stafford if he set foot on tribal land. Another tribe captured Stafford. But he convinced them that he wasn't a threat. Luckily, most people he met on his journey were happy to help him.

A Disappearing Forest

6   The long river that Stafford trekked passes through the Amazon rainforest. The rainforest typically receives more than 100 inches of rainfall a year. Along the way, Stafford saw large areas of demolished forest.

7   About 30 million people live in the Amazon region. But this area is in trouble. Loggers have cut down vast areas of the rainforest. They have been selling the wood and making room for homes, roads, and farms. So far, more than 20 percent of the rainforest has been destroyed.

8   This clearing of trees is called deforestation. Cutting down trees has threatened many plants and animals. The Amazon rainforest is home to more species of plants and animals than any other place in the world. In fact, more than 100,000 types of insects live there. People all over the world rely on the rainforest for food and medicines made from its plants.

9   In addition, trees in rainforests absorb carbon dioxide from the air and release oxygen. Carbon dioxide is a gas that traps heat in the atmosphere. As forests disappear, more of this gas remains in the atmosphere. Experts say that too much carbon dioxide is causing temperatures to slowly rise around the world.

10   Brazil has put part of the Amazon rainforest under government protection. In 2012, the number of trees cut down in Brazil's rainforest dropped to its lowest level in 20 years.

Spreading the Word

11   People like Stafford are helping the cause too. He has seen the importance of protecting rainforests up close. During his long journey, he carried a laptop so he could blog about his experiences.

12   "The rainforest is so important. The planet won't survive without large forests," he says. "It's **vital** that people realize that deforestation is still going on. The rainforest can't continue to shrink and shrink. The more people who care about the Amazon, the better."

Name: _____

Directions: Read the article "Walking the Amazon." Then answer the questions below.

1. **What does the word *vital* mean as it is used in paragraph 12?**

   A. Hard to believe

   B. Depressing

   C. Very important

   D. Understandable

2. **Which sentence from the article best supports the answer to question 1?**

   A. Brazil has put part of the Amazon rainforest under government protection. *(paragraph 10)*

   B. "The planet won't survive without large forests," he says. *(paragraph 12)*

   C. During his long journey, he carried a laptop so he could blog about his experiences. *(paragraph 11)*

   D. In addition, trees in rainforests absorb carbon dioxide from the air and release oxygen. *(paragraph 9)*

3. **What are two main ideas found in the article? (Select two choices.)**

   A. Ed Stafford walked the length of the Amazon River.

   B. Brazil has taken steps to protect the Amazon rainforest.

   C. The Amazon is home to many different insects.

   D. The Amazon rainforest is in danger.

   E. It is not safe to cross into tribal territory.

   F. The Amazon is an interesting place to visit.

Ed Stafford with Cho Rivera

4. **In the section "A Disappearing Forest," how does the author support the idea that the Amazon is in trouble?**

   A. The author tells a story using firsthand observations of the rainforest.

   B. The author explains a problem and then presents various solutions.

   C. The author details the main cause and effects of deforestation.

   D. The author compares Brazil's approach to the problem with the approaches of other countries.

5. **How does the final paragraph relate to the first paragraph?**

   A. It clarifies that deforestation was the cause of the obstacles Stafford faced.

   B. It reveals a big part of Stafford's motivation for making such a difficult trip.

   C. It explains why the journey took as long as it did.

   D. It implies that Stafford has regrets about his adventure.

6. **On a separate sheet of paper, explain why Stafford's adventure was a challenging one. Provide at least two details to support your answer.**

Scholastic News Leveled Informational Texts (Grade 5) © Scholastic Inc.

Walking the Amazon

1   Imagine encountering 20-foot-long snakes and caiman crocodiles, and facing the constant threat of drowning. That is exactly what happened to Ed Stafford. He went on a 2½-year journey along the Amazon River in South America.

2   In August 2010, Stafford became the first person to trek the entire length of the Amazon River. Stafford is from England. He wanted to do something that had never been done before. And he wanted to see the problems facing the Amazon region firsthand.

From Source to Sea

3   On April 2, 2008, Stafford began his journey at the source of the Amazon River, in Peru. From there, the river travels 4,200 miles eastward. It empties into the Atlantic Ocean in Maruda, Brazil. In August 2008, a guide, Gadiel "Cho" Sánchez Rivera, joined Stafford. On August 9, 2010, Stafford jumped into the ocean with Cho to celebrate finally reaching the end. Stafford had walked for 859 days.

4   It was a well-deserved celebration. Along the way, Stafford wore out several pairs of shoes. But that was the least of his problems. He braved stings from hundreds of wasps and bites from thousands of mosquitoes. He waded in water filled with electric eels and dodged snakes and scorpions. He also faced starvation.

5   That's not all. The chief of a native tribe in Peru said he'd kill Stafford if he set foot on tribal land. Another tribe captured Stafford, but he convinced them that he wasn't a threat. Luckily, most people he met on his journey were happy to help him.

A Disappearing Forest

6   The long river that Stafford trekked winds through the Amazon rainforest. A rainforest is a forest located in a region that typically receives more than 100 inches of rainfall a year. Along the way, Stafford saw large areas of demolished forest.

7   About 30 million people live in the Amazon region. But this area is in trouble. Loggers have cut down vast areas of the rainforest to sell the wood and to make room for homes, roads, and farms. So far, more than 20 percent of the rainforest has been destroyed.

8   This clearing of trees, called deforestation, has threatened many plants and animals. The Amazon rainforest is home to more species of plants and animals than any other place in the world. In fact, more than 100,000 types of insects live there. People worldwide rely on the rainforest for food and medicines made from its plants.

9   In addition, trees in rainforests absorb carbon dioxide from the air and release oxygen. Carbon dioxide is a gas that traps heat in the atmosphere. As forests disappear, more of this gas remains in the atmosphere. Experts say that too much carbon dioxide is causing temperatures worldwide to slowly rise.

10   Brazil has put part of the Amazon rainforest under government protection. In 2012, the number of trees cut down in Brazil's rainforest dropped to its lowest level in 20 years.

Spreading the Word

11   People like Stafford are helping the cause too. He has seen the importance of protecting rainforests up close. During his long journey, he carried a laptop so he could blog about his experiences.

12   "The rainforest is so important. The planet won't survive without large forests," he says. "It's **vital** that people realize that deforestation is still going on. The rainforest can't continue to shrink and shrink. The more people who care about the Amazon, the better."

Name: _____

Directions: Read the article "Walking the Amazon." Then answer the questions below.

1. **What does the word *vital* mean as it is used in paragraph 12?**

   A. Essential

   B. Understandable

   C. Depressing

   D. Unbelievable

2. **Which sentence from the article best supports the answer to question 1?**

   A. In addition, trees in rainforests absorb carbon dioxide from the air and release oxygen. *(paragraph 9)*

   B. Brazil has put part of the Amazon rainforest under government protection. *(paragraph 10)*

   C. "The planet won't survive without large forests," he says. *(paragraph 12)*

   D. During his long journey, he carried a laptop so he could blog about his experiences. *(paragraph 11)*

3. **What are two main ideas found in the article? (Select two choices.)**

   A. Brazil has taken steps to protect the Amazon rainforest.

   B. Ed Stafford walked the length of the Amazon River.

   C. The Amazon is home to many different insects.

   D. It is not safe to cross into tribal territory.

   E. The Amazon is an interesting place to visit.

   F. The Amazon rainforest is in danger.

Ed Stafford with Cho Rivera

4. **In the section "A Disappearing Forest," how does the author support the idea that the Amazon is in trouble?**

   A. The author explains a problem and then presents various solutions.

   B. The author details the main cause and effects of deforestation.

   C. The author tells a story using firsthand observations of the rainforest.

   D. The author compares Brazil's approach to the problem with the approaches of other countries.

5. **How does the final paragraph relate to the first paragraph?**

   A. It reveals a big part of Stafford's motivation for making such a difficult trip.

   B. It clarifies that deforestation was the cause of the obstacles Stafford faced.

   C. It implies that Stafford has regrets about his adventure.

   D. It explains why the journey took as long as it did.

6. **On a separate sheet of paper, explain why Stafford's adventure was a challenging one. Provide at least two details to support your answer.**

Scholastic News Leveled Informational Texts (Grade 5) © Scholastic Inc.

Walking the Amazon

1　Imagine encountering 20-foot-long snakes and caiman crocodiles, and facing the constant threat of drowning. That is exactly what happened to Ed Stafford on his 2½-year journey along the Amazon River in South America.

2　In August 2010, Stafford became the first person to trek the entire length of the Amazon River. Stafford, who is from England, wanted to do something that had never been done—and see the problems facing the Amazon region firsthand.

From Source to Sea

3　On April 2, 2008, Stafford began his journey at the source of the Amazon River, in Peru. From there, the river travels 4,200 miles eastward, emptying into the Atlantic Ocean in Maruda, Brazil. In August 2008, Stafford was joined by a guide, Gadiel "Cho" Sánchez Rivera. On August 9, 2010, after 859 days of walking, Stafford jumped into the ocean with Cho to celebrate finally reaching the end.

4　It was a well-deserved celebration. Along the way, Stafford wore out several pairs of shoes. But that was the least of his problems. He braved stings from hundreds of wasps and bites from thousands of mosquitoes. He also faced starvation, waded in water filled with electric eels, and dodged snakes and scorpions.

5　That's not all. The chief of a native tribe in Peru said he'd kill Stafford if he set foot on tribal land. Another tribe captured Stafford, but he convinced them that he wasn't a threat. Luckily, most people he met on his journey were happy to help him.

A Disappearing Forest

6　The long river that Stafford trekked winds through the Amazon rainforest. A rainforest is a forest located in a region that typically receives more than 100 inches of rainfall a year. Along the way, Stafford encountered large areas of demolished forest.

7　The Amazon region, where about 30 million people live, is in trouble. Loggers have cut down vast areas of the rainforest to sell the wood and to make room for homes, roads, and farms. So far, more than 20 percent of the rainforest has been destroyed.

8　This clearing of trees, called deforestation, has threatened many plants and animals. The Amazon rainforest is home to more species of plants and animals than any other place in the world. In fact, more than 100,000 types of insects live there. People worldwide rely on the rainforest for food and medicines made from its plants.

9　In addition, trees in rainforests absorb carbon dioxide from the air and release oxygen. Carbon dioxide is a gas that traps heat in the atmosphere. As forests disappear, more of this gas remains in the atmosphere. Experts say that too much carbon dioxide is causing temperatures worldwide to slowly rise.

10　Brazil has put part of the Amazon rainforest under government protection. In 2012, the number of trees cut down in Brazil's rainforest dropped to its lowest level in 20 years.

Spreading the Word

11　People like Stafford are helping the cause too. He has seen the importance of protecting rainforests up close. During his long journey, he carried a laptop so he could blog about his experiences.

12　"The rainforest is so important. The planet won't survive without large forests," he says. "It's **vital** that people realize that deforestation is still going on. The rainforest can't continue to shrink and shrink. The more people who care about the Amazon, the better."

Scholastic News Leveled Informational Texts (Grade 5) © Scholastic Inc.

Name: _____

Directions: Read the article "Walking the Amazon." Then answer the questions below.

1. **What does the word *vital* mean as it is used in paragraph 12?**

    A. Depressing   C. Unbelievable

    B. Understandable   D. Crucial

2. **Which sentence from the article best supports the answer to question 1?**

    A. "The planet won't survive without large forests," he says. *(paragraph 12)*

    B. Brazil has put part of the Amazon rainforest under government protection. *(paragraph 10)*

    C. During his long journey, he carried a laptop so he could blog about his experiences. *(paragraph 11)*

    D. In addition, trees in rainforests absorb carbon dioxide from the air and release oxygen. *(paragraph 9)*

3. **What are two main ideas found in the article? (Select two choices.)**

    A. Brazil has taken steps to protect the Amazon rainforest.

    B. The Amazon is home to many different insects.

    C. The Amazon rainforest is in danger.

    D. It is not safe to cross into tribal territory.

    E. Ed Stafford walked the length of the Amazon River.

    F. The Amazon is an interesting place to visit.

Ed Stafford with Cho Rivera

4. **In the section "A Disappearing Forest," how does the author support the idea that the Amazon is in trouble?**

    A. The author details the main cause and effects of deforestation.

    B. The author explains a problem and then presents various solutions.

    C. The author compares Brazil's approach to the problem with the approaches of other countries.

    D. The author tells a story using firsthand observations of the rainforest.

5. **How does the final paragraph relate to the first paragraph?**

    A. It clarifies that deforestation was the cause of the obstacles Stafford faced.

    B. It explains why the journey took as long as it did.

    C. It implies that Stafford has regrets about his adventure.

    D. It reveals a big part of Stafford's motivation for making such a difficult trip.

6. **On a separate sheet of paper, explain why Stafford's adventure was a challenging one. Provide at least two details to support your answer.**

Invasion of the Drones

1   It was just after 3 a.m. on January 26, 2015. A Secret Service officer was patrolling the White House lawn. Suddenly, he noticed a suspicious object flying just above the ground. It was about 2 feet wide and had four small propellers, like those on a helicopter. The White House went on high alert. The object crashed into a tree, and officials rushed to check it out. The flying machine was a remote-controlled aircraft. It was a drone, or unmanned aerial vehicle (UAV).

2   Luckily, the drone wasn't being used to harm anyone. It was just an expensive toy that had gotten away from someone who was flying it nearby. No one was injured. But the incident raised some serious questions about drones. It's the latest chapter in an ongoing debate: Are these unmanned aircraft useful tools or are they a threat to our safety and privacy?

Drones All Around Us

3   The U.S. military first used drones in the 1930s. Pilots and gunners used them for target practice. They would shoot the flying machines out of the sky. Today, the military is still the leading user of drones. (See "Drones in War," next page.) But companies are also making smaller, cheaper drones for civilians. People can buy UAVs online for as little as $500.

4   Drones with cameras can be used in many innovative ways. Movie directors use them to film scenes from a bird's-eye view. Farmers use them to monitor their crops and livestock. Scientists recently used drones to count and study sea lions in Alaska. Drones can also help the police in rescue missions or search for suspected criminals.

Someday, drones may even deliver packages or pizza to your door.

The Drone Debate

5   As drones become more popular, people become more concerned about safety. Drones can be difficult to control. People have lost control of them because of wind gusts and software glitches. Many end up smashing into trees or buildings.

6   Drones have also come very close to colliding with passenger planes. In 2015, pilots reported more than 1,000 drone sightings. Many were above 400 feet, the highest a drone is allowed to go. A drone could get sucked into an airplane's engine. That could cause the plane to crash.

7   Many legal experts are also concerned. They say drones with cameras could be used to spy on people.

8   "Someone could fly them around the neighborhood," says Hillary Farber. "They could capture images of people in their backyards." Farber is a professor at the University of Massachusetts School of Law.

This drone is similar to the one that crashed onto the White House lawn.

9   The Federal Aviation Administration (FAA) regulates the use of non-military aircraft in the United States. Recently, the FAA set new rules for the use of drones. It also created a national drone registry, or list. People who buy drones now have to register them. This will help officials track down the owner of a drone that flies anywhere it shouldn't.

10   "It's all about finding balance," says Farber. "How are we going to use [drones] in a way that's safe and not invading people's privacy?"

Drones in War

11   Drones are playing a bigger role in warfare than ever before. Nearly one in three U.S. military aircraft is a UAV. Some are the size of large model airplanes. Others are as big as a small jet. They can hold up to 3,000 pounds of missiles and bombs.

12   The U.S. has used drones to attack suspected terrorists in places like Afghanistan and Iraq.

13   UAVs have some advantages over piloted aircraft. They can stay in the air for days. They can also keep pilots safe from the dangers of the battlefield. The military says drone strikes are very precise.

14   But human rights groups say many drone attacks have accidentally killed civilians. Critics also say drones make war seem more like a video game, not a real life-and-death situation.

A U.S. Air Force drone called the RQ-4 Global Hawk

Name: _____

Directions: Read the article "Invasion of the Drones." Then answer the questions below.

1. According to the article, people are debating whether drones ____.

   A. should be banned

   B. are a threat to people's safety and privacy

   C. are too expensive

   D. should be used only for target practice

2. Which of the following would the author probably <u>not</u> consider to be an innovative use of drones?

   A. Flying drones for fun

   B. Helping rescue pets

   C. Filming scenes from dramatic angles

   D. Keeping track of the number of sea lions in Alaska

3. Why is Hillary Farber concerned about the use of drones?

   A. The commercial regulation of drones is too strict.

   B. The environmental laws regarding drones are unclear.

   C. The popularity of drones is declining.

   D. The use of drones could invade people's privacy.

4. Which sentence from the article best supports the answer to question 3?

   A. Pilots and gunners used them for target practice. *(paragraph 3)*

   B. They say drones with cameras could be used to spy on people. *(paragraph 7)*

   C. Recently, the FAA set new rules for the use of drones. *(paragraph 9)*

   D. People have lost control of them because of wind gusts and software glitches. *(paragraph 5)*

5. What is the sidebar "Drones in War" mostly about?

   A. The history of how drones have been used in war

   B. The ways filmmakers use drones to realistically portray war

   C. How drones are being used in modern warfare

   D. How drones are used to create video games with war scenes

6. In the article, Professor Hillary Farber talks about "finding balance" in the use of drones. What do you think she means? Do you think the FAA is working to find a balance? Explain on a separate sheet of paper, using details from the article.

Invasion of the Drones

1   It was just after 3 a.m. on January 26, 2015. A Secret Service officer was patrolling the White House lawn. Suddenly, he noticed a suspicious object flying just above the ground. It was about 2 feet wide and had four small propellers, like those on a helicopter. The White House went on high alert. The object crashed into a tree, and officials rushed to check it out. The flying machine was a remote-controlled aircraft known as a drone, or unmanned aerial vehicle (UAV).

2   Luckily, the drone wasn't being used to harm anyone. It was just an expensive toy that had gotten away from someone who was flying it nearby. No one was injured. But the incident raised some serious questions about drones. It's the latest chapter in an ongoing debate: Are these unmanned aircraft useful tools or are they a threat to our safety and privacy?

Drones All Around Us

3   The U.S. military first used drones in the 1930s. Pilots and gunners used them for target practice. They shot them out of the sky. Today, the military remains the leading user of drones. (See "Drones in War," next page.) But companies have also begun making smaller, cheaper drones for civilians. UAVs, like the one that crashed at the White House, can be bought online for as little as $500.

4   Drones equipped with cameras are being used in many innovative ways. Movie directors use drones to film scenes from a bird's-eye view. Farmers use them to monitor the health of their crops and livestock. Scientists recently used drones to count and study sea lions in Alaska.

5   Drones can be an effective tool for law enforcement too. Police departments use drones to assist with rescue missions or search for suspected criminals. Drones may even be arriving at your doorstep in the future. Amazon, the online retail store, hopes to use drones to deliver packages someday. Domino's recently tested delivering pizzas using drones.

6   "The uses are limited only by the imagination," says Colin Guinn. He works for 3D Robotics, a major U.S. drone manufacturer.

The Drone Debate

7   The increased popularity of drones has raised safety concerns. Drones can be difficult to control. People have lost control of them because of wind gusts and software glitches. Most of these "flyaways" end with the drones smashing into trees or buildings.

8   Drones have also come dangerously close to colliding with passenger planes. The Federal Aviation Administration (FAA) oversees the use of non-military aircraft in the United States. In 2015, it said that pilots had reported more than 1,000 drone sightings. Many were above 400 feet—the highest a drone is allowed to go. Many people fear that a drone could get sucked

This drone is similar to the one that crashed onto the White House lawn.

into the engine of an airplane. That could cause the plane to crash.

9   In addition, many legal experts are concerned that drones with cameras could be used to invade people's privacy.

10   "Someone could fly them around the neighborhood and capture images of people in their backyards," says Hillary Farber. She is a professor at the University of Massachusetts School of Law. Farber has written about privacy issues related to drones.

11   Many people are also worried that the government and the police could use drones to spy on citizens.

12   Recently, the FAA created new rules for the use of drones. It also created a national drone registry, or list. That means people have to register drones when they buy them. The registry will help officials track down the owner of a drone that flies anywhere it shouldn't.

13   "It's all about finding balance," says Farber. "How are we going to use [drones] in a way that's safe and not invading people's privacy?"

Drones in War

14   Drones are playing a bigger role in warfare than ever before. In fact, nearly one in three U.S. military aircraft is an unmanned aerial vehicle (UAV). Some are the size of large model airplanes. Others are as big as a small jet and can hold up to 3,000 pounds of missiles and bombs.

15   Operators use joysticks to control drones thousands of miles away. They sit in front of video screens at military bases in the U.S. The U.S. has used drones to attack hundreds of suspected terrorists in places like Afghanistan and Iraq.

16   Drones have some advantages over piloted aircraft. They can stay in the air for days. They can also keep pilots from having to face the dangers of the battlefield. The military says UAV strikes are very precise.

17   But the use of military UAVs has created controversy as well. Human rights groups argue that many drone attacks have accidentally killed civilians. Critics also say drones make war seem more like a video game rather than a real life-and-death situation.

A U.S. Air Force drone called the RQ-4 Global Hawk

Name: _____

Directions: Read the article "Invasion of the Drones." Then answer the questions below.

1. **According to the article, people are debating whether drones ____.**

   A. should be used only for target practice

   B. are too expensive

   C. are a threat to people's safety and privacy

   D. should be banned

2. **Which of the following would the author probably <u>not</u> consider to be an innovative use of drones?**

   A. Helping rescue pets

   B. Keeping track of the number of sea lions in Alaska

   C. Filming scenes from dramatic angles

   D. Flying drones for fun

3. **Why is Hillary Farber concerned about the use of drones?**

   A. The use of drones could invade people's privacy.

   B. The environmental laws regarding drones are unclear.

   C. The popularity of drones is declining.

   D. The commercial regulation of drones is too strict.

4. **Which sentence from the article best supports the answer to question 3?**

   A. Many people are also worried that the government and the police could use drones to spy on citizens. *(paragraph 11)*

   B. People have lost control of them because of wind gusts and software glitches. *(paragraph 7)*

   C. Recently, the FAA created new rules for the use of drones. *(paragraph 12)*

   D. Pilots and gunners used them for target practice. *(paragraph 3)*

5. **What is the sidebar "Drones in War" mostly about?**

   A. The history of how drones have been used in war

   B. How drones are being used in modern warfare

   C. How drones are used to create video games with war scenes

   D. The ways filmmakers use drones to realistically portray war

6. **In the article, Professor Hillary Farber talks about "finding balance" in the use of drones. What do you think she means? Do you think the FAA is working to find a balance? Explain on a separate sheet of paper, using details from the article.**

Invasion of the Drones

1   It was just after 3 a.m. on January 26, 2015. A Secret Service officer was patrolling the White House lawn when he noticed a suspicious object flying just above the ground. It was about 2 feet wide and had four small propellers like those on a helicopter. The White House went on high alert. After the object crashed into a tree, officials rushed to check it out. The unwelcome flying machine was a remote-controlled aircraft known as a drone, or unmanned aerial vehicle (UAV).

2   Luckily, the drone wasn't being used to harm anyone. It was just an expensive toy that had gotten away from someone who was flying it nearby. No one was injured, but the incident raised some serious questions about drones. It's the latest chapter in the debate over whether these unmanned aircraft are useful tools or a threat to our safety and privacy.

Drones All Around Us

3   The U.S. military first used drones in the 1930s. Pilots and gunners used them for target practice, shooting them out of the sky. Today, the military remains the leading user of drones. (See "Drones in War," next page.) But companies have also begun making smaller, cheaper drones that civilians can fly. For example, UAVs like the one that crashed onto the White House lawn can be bought online for as little as $500.

4   Drones equipped with cameras are being used in many innovative ways. Movie directors use drones to film scenes from a bird's-eye view. Farmers use them to monitor the health of their crops and livestock. And scientists recently used drones to count and study sea lions in Alaska.

5   Law-enforcement officials say drones can be an effective tool for them too. Police departments have purchased drones to assist with rescue missions or search for suspected criminals. Drones may even be arriving at your doorstep in the future. Amazon, the online retail store, hopes to use drones to deliver packages to customers someday. Domino's recently tested delivering pizzas using drones.

6   "The uses are limited only by the imagination," says Colin Guinn. He works for 3D Robotics, a major U.S. drone manufacturer.

The Drone Debate

7   The increased popularity of drones has raised safety concerns. Drones can be difficult to control. Wind gusts and software glitches have caused people to lose control of them. Most of these "flyaways"—like the one at the White House—end with the drones smashing into trees or buildings.

This drone is similar to the one that crashed onto the White House lawn.

Scholastic News Leveled Informational Texts (Grade 5) © Scholastic Inc.

8   But drones have also come dangerously close to colliding with passenger planes. The Federal Aviation Administration (FAA) oversees the use of non-military aircraft in the United States. In 2015, it said that pilots had reported more than 1,000 drone sightings. Many were above 400 feet—the highest a drone is allowed to go. Many people fear that a drone could get sucked into the engine of an airliner, causing it to crash.

9   In addition, many legal experts are concerned that drones with cameras could be used to invade people's privacy.

10   "Someone could fly them around the neighborhood and capture images of people in their backyards," says Hillary Farber. She is a professor at the University of Massachusetts School of Law who has written about privacy issues related to drones.

11   Many people are also worried that the government and the police could use drones to spy on citizens.

12   Recently, the FAA created new rules for the use of drones. It also created a national drone registry, or list. That means people have to register drones when they buy them. The registry will help officials track down the owner of a drone that flies anywhere it shouldn't.

13   "It's all about finding balance," says Farber. "How are we going to use [drones] in a way that's safe and not invading people's privacy?"

Drones in War

14   Drones are playing a bigger role in warfare than ever before. In fact, nearly one in three U.S. military aircraft is an unmanned aerial vehicle (UAV). Some are the size of large model airplanes. Others are as big as a small jet and can hold up to 3,000 pounds of missiles and bombs.

15   Sitting in front of video screens at military bases in the U.S., drone operators use joysticks to control drones thousands of miles away. Since 2002, the U.S. has used drones to attack hundreds of suspected terrorists in places like Afghanistan and Iraq.

16   Drones have some advantages over piloted aircraft. They can stay in the air for days, and they keep pilots from having to face the dangers of the battlefield. The military says UAV strikes are very precise.

17   But the use of military UAVs has created controversy as well. Human rights groups argue that many drone attacks have accidentally killed civilians. Critics also say drones make war seem more like a video game rather than a real life-and-death situation.

A U.S. Air Force drone called the RQ-4 Global Hawk

Name: _____

Directions: Read the article "Invasion of the Drones." Then answer the questions below.

1. **According to the article, people are debating whether drones ____.**

   A. are too expensive

   B. should be used only for target practice

   C. should be banned

   D. are a threat to people's safety and privacy

2. **Which of the following would the author probably <u>not</u> consider to be an innovative use of drones?**

   A. Filming scenes from dramatic angles

   B. Keeping track of the number of sea lions in Alaska

   C. Flying drones for fun

   D. Helping rescue pets

3. **Why is Hillary Farber concerned about the use of drones?**

   A. The environmental laws regarding drones are unclear.

   B. The popularity of drones is declining.

   C. The use of drones could invade people's privacy.

   D. The commercial regulation of drones is too strict.

4. **Which sentence from the article best supports the answer to question 3?**

   A. Wind gusts and software glitches have caused people to lose control of them. *(paragraph 7)*

   B. Recently, the FAA created new rules for the use of drones. *(paragraph 12)*

   C. Pilots and gunners used them for target practice, shooting them out of the sky. *(paragraph 3)*

   D. Many people are also worried that the government and the police could use drones to spy on citizens. *(paragraph 11)*

5. **What is the sidebar "Drones in War" mostly about?**

   A. How drones are being used in modern warfare

   B. The history of how drones have been used in war

   C. The ways filmmakers use drones to realistically portray war

   D. How drones are used to create video games with war scenes

6. **In the article, Professor Hillary Farber talks about "finding balance" in the use of drones. What do you think she means? Do you think the FAA is working to find a balance? Explain on a separate sheet of paper, using details from the article.**

A Battle Over Bags

1   Shawntil Bailey had just finished shopping at a supermarket in Austin, Texas. She was carrying a paper bag filled with groceries. Suddenly, the bag ripped. Her groceries went crashing to the ground.

2   "I've lost loads of groceries lots of times," Bailey says. "The paper bags aren't as sturdy as the plastic ones."

3   So why doesn't Bailey get plastic bags? Because it's against the law. Since March 2013, stores in Austin cannot give out disposable plastic bags at checkout counters. Instead, they give out paper bags. Store shoppers can also bring their own reusable cloth bags.

4   A growing number of places in the United States have banned plastic shopping bags. In January 2013, Los Angeles became the largest U.S. city to ban the bags. The same month, the Big Island of Hawaii adopted a similar law. Plastic bags are now banned everywhere in the state.

5   Why the ban? Officials say they're trying to cut down on garbage and protect oceans and wildlife. Will other cities and states follow their lead?

Plastic Problems

6   Americans use a lot of plastic bags. They use about 100 billion of them each year, according to the U.S. International Trade Commission. Most plastic bags end up in landfills. They get buried with other trash under layers of dirt. Some experts say the bags may take up to 1,000 years to decompose, or break down, in landfills.

7   But many plastic bags never make it to landfills. Instead, they become litter on the street. They may wash down sewer drains or blow into rivers and oceans. In the water, the bags can hurt marine animals. Fish, sea turtles, and seabirds can get caught in the bags. They might even mistake the bags for food and choke on them.

8   All these environmental problems have made plastic bags a target worldwide. At least six countries, including China and Italy, have banned them.

9   "The sheer number of plastic bags in the environment means that they're going to have a **detrimental** impact," says Robert Harris. He is the director of the Hawaii chapter of the Sierra Club, an environmental group.

Bag the Ban?

10   But many people think plastic bags are getting a bad rap. Phil Rozenski works for Hilex Poly. It is the largest manufacturer of plastic bags in the U.S. He says people often reuse plastic bags for other purposes. A survey by the American Chemistry Council showed that 9 out of 10 people reuse plastic bags. They might use the bags to line trash cans, store items, and more. In addition, billions of the bags are recycled each year.

11   Rozenski argues that plastic-bag bans may also cost many Americans their jobs. He says the plastic-bag industry employs 30,000 people.

12   "Thirty thousand families are pretty important," he says.

Changing Behavior

13   For now, people who live in places where plastic bags have been banned are learning to get along without them.

14   Olga Garcia also lives in Austin. She now brings reusable bags with her to the grocery store.

15   "When the ban first happened, I was upset," she says. "But it feels better now, because I'm not wasting any bags."

Scholastic News Leveled Informational Texts (Grade 5) © Scholastic Inc.

Name: _____

Directions: Read the article "A Battle Over Bags." Then answer the questions below.

1. Which of the following points does the author make in this article?

    A. U.S. cities and states aren't the only places in the world trying to stop the problems caused by plastic bags.

    B. Almost every U.S. state has banned the use of plastic bags.

    C. No one wants to stop using plastic bags.

    D. Every state should make recycling plastic bags a law.

2. Which sentence from the article best supports the answer to question 1?

    A. A growing number of places in the United States have banned plastic shopping bags. *(paragraph 4)*

    B. For now, people who live in places where plastic bags have been banned are learning to get along without them. *(paragraph 13)*

    C. At least six countries, including China and Italy, have banned them. *(paragraph 8)*

    D. In addition, billions of the bags are recycled each year. *(paragraph 10)*

3. What does the word *detrimental* mean as it is used in paragraph 9?

    A. Important

    B. Helpful

    C. Harmful

    D. Costly

4. Which sentence from the article best supports the answer to question 3?

    A. "The paper bags aren't as sturdy as the plastic ones." *(paragraph 2)*

    B. In the water, the bags can hurt marine animals. *(paragraph 7)*

    C. But many people think plastic bags are getting a bad rap. *(paragraph 10)*

    D. Rozenski argues that plastic-bag bans may also cost many Americans their jobs. *(paragraph 11)*

5. How does the section "Bag the Ban?" contribute to the development of ideas in the article?

    A. It describes the effects of plastic bags on the environment.

    B. It makes comparisons between plastic bags and paper bags.

    C. It summarizes the reasons people want to ban plastic bags.

    D. It presents the point of view of those who think banning plastic bags is not necessary.

Name: _____

6. **All of the following reasons support the point of view presented in the section "Bag the Ban?" except that _____.**

   A. the plastic-bag industry provides jobs to thousands of Americans

   B. the plastic-bag industry makes generous contributions to environmental groups

   C. plastic bags are reused by most people

   D. billions of bags are recycled each year

7. **What do you think should be the law regarding plastic bags in your town or city? Explain your opinion, using details from the article to support your answer.**

_____

_____

_____

_____

_____

_____

_____

_____

_____

_____

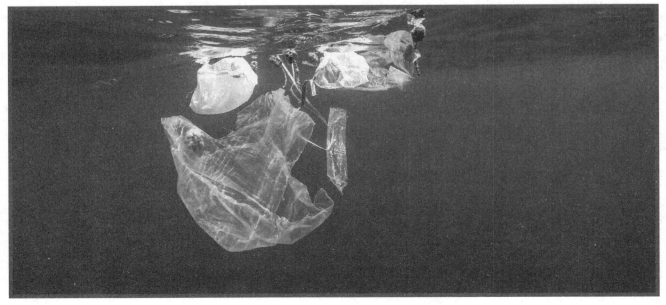

Scholastic News Leveled Informational Texts (Grade 5) © Scholastic Inc.

A Battle Over Bags

1   Shawntil Bailey was carrying a paper bag filled with groceries out of a supermarket in Austin, Texas. Suddenly, the bag ripped. Her groceries went crashing to the ground.

2   "I've lost loads of groceries lots of times," Bailey says. "The paper bags aren't as sturdy as the plastic ones."

3   Bailey isn't the only person in Austin who's had to adjust to life without plastic bags. Since March 2013, stores in Austin cannot give out disposable plastic bags at checkout counters. Instead, they give out paper bags. Store shoppers can also bring their own reusable cloth bags.

4   A growing number of places in the United States have banned plastic shopping bags. In January 2013, Los Angeles became the largest U.S. city to ban the bags. The same month, the Big Island of Hawaii adopted a similar law. Plastic bags are now banned everywhere in the state.

5   Why the ban? Officials say they're trying to cut down on garbage and protect oceans and wildlife. Will other cities and states follow their lead?

Plastic Problems

6   Americans use a lot of plastic bags. They use about 100 billion of them each year, according to the U.S. International Trade Commission. Most plastic bags end up in landfills. They get buried with other trash under layers of dirt. Some experts say the bags may take up to 1,000 years to decompose, or break down, in landfills.

7   But many plastic bags never make it to landfills. Instead, they become litter on the street. They may wash down sewer drains or blow into rivers and oceans. Once in the water, the bags pose a threat to marine animals. Fish, sea turtles, and seabirds can get caught in the bags. They might even mistake the bags for food and choke on them.

8   All these environmental problems have made plastic bags a target worldwide. At least six countries, including China and Italy, have banned them.

9   "The sheer number of plastic bags in the environment means that they're going to have a **detrimental** impact," says Robert Harris. He is the director of the Hawaii chapter of the Sierra Club, an environmental group.

Bag the Ban?

10   Many people, however, think plastic bags are getting a bad rap. Phil Rozenski works for Hilex Poly, the largest U.S. plastic-bag manufacturer. He says plastic bags are often reused for other purposes. A survey by the American Chemistry Council showed that 9 out of 10 people reuse plastic bags. They might use the bags to line trash cans, store items, and more. In addition, billions of the bags are recycled each year.

11   Rozenski argues that plastic-bag bans may also cost many Americans their jobs. He says that the plastic-bag industry employs 30,000 people.

12   "Thirty thousand families are pretty important," he says.

Changing Behavior

13   For now, people who live in places where plastic bags have been banned are learning to get along without them.

14   Olga Garcia also lives in Austin. She says she now brings reusable bags with her to the grocery store.

15   "When the ban first happened, I was upset," she says. "But it feels better now, because I'm not wasting any bags."

Name: _____

Directions: Read the article "A Battle Over Bags." Then answer the questions below.

1. Which of the following points does the author make in this article?

   A. Almost every U.S. state has banned the use of plastic bags.

   B. U.S. cities and states aren't the only places in the world trying to stop the problems caused by plastic bags.

   C. No one wants to stop using plastic bags.

   D. Every state should make recycling plastic bags a law.

2. Which sentence from the article best supports the answer to question 1?

   A. In addition, billions of the bags are recycled each year. *(paragraph 10)*

   B. A growing number of places in the United States have banned plastic shopping bags. *(paragraph 4)*

   C. For now, people who live in places where plastic bags have been banned are learning to get along without them. *(paragraph 13)*

   D. At least six countries, including China and Italy, have banned them. *(paragraph 8)*

3. What does the word *detrimental* mean as it is used in paragraph 9?

   A. Harmful

   B. Important

   C. Helpful

   D. Costly

4. Which sentence from the article best supports the answer to question 3?

   A. Rozenski argues that plastic-bag bans may also cost many Americans their jobs. *(paragraph 11)*

   B. "The paper bags aren't as sturdy as the plastic ones." *(paragraph 2)*

   C. Many people, however, think plastic bags are getting a bad rap. *(paragraph 10)*

   D. Once in the water, the bags pose a threat to marine animals. *(paragraph 7)*

5. How does the section "Bag the Ban?" contribute to the development of ideas in the article?

   A. It presents the point of view of those who think banning plastic bags is not necessary.

   B. It describes the effects of plastic bags on the environment.

   C. It makes comparisons between plastic bags and paper bags.

   D. It summarizes the reasons people want to ban plastic bags.

6. All of the following reasons support the point of view presented in the section "Bag the Ban?" except that _____.

    A. billions of bags are recycled each year

    B. plastic bags are reused by most people

    C. the plastic-bag industry makes generous contributions to environmental groups

    D. the plastic-bag industry provides jobs to thousands of Americans

7. What do you think should be the law regarding plastic bags in your town or city? Explain your opinion, using details from the article to support your answer.

_____

_____

_____

_____

_____

_____

_____

_____

_____

_____

A Battle Over Bags

1   Shawntil Bailey was carrying a paper bag filled with groceries out of a supermarket in Austin, Texas. Suddenly, the bag ripped. Her groceries went crashing to the ground.

2   "I've lost loads of groceries lots of times," Bailey says. "The paper bags aren't as sturdy as the plastic ones."

3   Bailey isn't the only person in the Texas capital who's had to adjust to life without plastic bags. Since March 2013, stores in Austin haven't been allowed to give out disposable plastic bags at checkout counters. Instead, shoppers have to use their own reusable cloth bags or paper bags given out by the store.

4   A growing number of places in the United States have implemented bans on plastic shopping bags. The movement got a big boost in January 2013. That's when Los Angeles became the largest U.S. city to ban the bags. The same month, the Big Island of Hawaii adopted a similar law. There are now bans on plastic bags everywhere in the state.

5   Officials in places that have banned plastic bags say they're trying to cut down on garbage and protect oceans and wildlife. Will other cities and states follow their lead?

Plastic Problems

6   Americans use a lot of plastic bags—about 100 billion of them each year, according to the U.S. International Trade Commission. Most plastic bags end up in landfills, where they're buried with other trash under layers of dirt. Some experts say the bags may take up to 1,000 years to decompose, or break down, in landfills.

7   But many plastic bags never make it to landfills. Instead, they become litter on the street, wash down sewer drains, or blow into rivers and oceans. Once in the water, the bags pose a threat to marine animals.

Fish, sea turtles, and seabirds can get caught in the bags or mistake them for food and choke on them.

8   All these environmental problems have made plastic bags a target worldwide. At least six countries, including China and Italy, have banned them.

9   "The sheer number of plastic bags in the environment means that they're going to have a **detrimental** impact," says Robert Harris. He is the director of the Hawaii chapter of the Sierra Club, an environmental group.

Bag the Ban?

10   Many people, however, think plastic bags are getting a bad rap. Phil Rozenski works for Hilex Poly, the largest U.S. plastic-bag manufacturer. He says plastic bags are often reused for other purposes. A survey by the American Chemistry Council showed that 9 out of 10 people reuse plastic bags for things like lining trash cans and storing items. In addition, billions of the bags are recycled each year.

11   Rozenski argues that plastic-bag bans may also end up costing many Americans their jobs. He says that the plastic-bag industry employs 30,000 people.

12   "Thirty thousand families are pretty important," he says.

Changing Behavior

13   For now, people who live in places where plastic bags have been banned are learning to get along without them.

14   Olga Garcia, who lives in Austin, says she now brings reusable bags with her to the grocery store.

15   "When the ban first happened, I was upset," she says. "But it feels better now, because I'm not wasting any bags."

Scholastic News Leveled Informational Texts (Grade 5) © Scholastic Inc.

Name: _____

Directions: Read the article "A Battle Over Bags." Then answer the questions below.

1. **Which of the following points does the author make in this article?**

   A. No one wants to stop using plastic bags.

   B. Almost every U.S. state has banned the use of plastic bags.

   C. Every state should make recycling plastic bags a law.

   D. U.S. cities and states aren't the only places in the world trying to stop the problems caused by plastic bags.

2. **Which sentence from the article best supports the answer to question 1?**

   A. For now, people who live in places where plastic bags have been banned are learning to get along without them. (*paragraph 13*)

   B. At least six countries, including China and Italy, have banned them. (*paragraph 8*)

   C. A growing number of places in the United States have implemented bans on plastic shopping bags. (*paragraph 4*)

   D. In addition, billions of the bags are recycled each year. (*paragraph 10*)

3. **What does the word *detrimental* mean as it is used in paragraph 9?**

   A. Helpful

   B. Harmful

   C. Costly

   D. Important

4. **Which sentence from the article best supports the answer to question 3?**

   A. "The paper bags aren't as sturdy as the plastic ones." (*paragraph 2*)

   B. Many people, however, think plastic bags are getting a bad rap. (*paragraph 10*)

   C. Once in the water, the bags pose a threat to marine animals. (*paragraph 7*)

   D. Rozenski argues that plastic-bag bans may also end up costing many Americans their jobs. (*paragraph 11*)

5. **How does the section "Bag the Ban?" contribute to the development of ideas in the article?**

   A. It makes comparisons between plastic bags and paper bags.

   B. It describes the effects of plastic bags on the environment.

   C. It presents the point of view of those who think banning plastic bags is not necessary.

   D. It summarizes the reasons people want to ban plastic bags.

Name: _____

6. All of the following reasons support the point of view presented in the section "Bag the Ban?" except that _____.

   A. plastic bags are reused by most people

   B. the plastic-bag industry provides jobs to thousands of Americans

   C. billions of bags are recycled each year

   D. the plastic-bag industry makes generous contributions to environmental groups

7. What do you think should be the law regarding plastic bags in your town or city? Explain your opinion, using details from the article to support your answer.

   _____

   _____

   _____

   _____

   _____

   _____

   _____

   _____

   _____

   _____

Keep It Down!

1   The ocean has never been a quiet place. Icebergs screech as they grind against each other. Whales bellow to one another over long distances. Some fish actually grunt to attract mates or scare off predators.

2   But now the world's waters are noisier than ever before. Deep-sea oil drilling, shipping, and other human activities are the reasons. Scientists think all that racket is creating trouble for marine mammals. These animals must be able to detect sounds to survive. Researchers are working to find ways to turn down the ocean's volume.

"Seeing" With Sound

3   The deep ocean gets very little light. This makes it hard for marine mammals to see. So dolphins, porpoises, and many types of whales use sound to help them find their way around. This is known as echolocation. (See "'Seeing' Down Deep," next page.)

4   Marine mammals also make sounds to communicate with one another. For example, some whales sing to attract mates. Dolphins call each other by whistles.

5   The ocean has excellent **acoustics**. That means sound travels farther and faster through water than through air. This allows marine animals to communicate over long distances. But that also means they could hear the sound of a ship or deep-sea oil drilling thousands of miles away. Scientists are worried all this extra noise may be harming animals.

Can You Hear Me?

6   Ships that use propellers make the most noise. They can be louder than a jet engine. Studies have found that sea mammals are raising and changing their voices to be heard over all that noise.

7   "It's like trying to talk to a friend across a noisy classroom," says Jason Gedamke. He's a scientist at the National Oceanic and Atmospheric Administration (NOAA).

8   All that noise probably makes it harder for marine mammals to listen for predators. They could also have difficulty hunting or finding mates. In addition, scientists have discovered that loud booms from ships can cause permanent injury. Some animals have lost their hearing.

Lowering the Volume

9   What's being done to help these animals? NOAA has been tracking levels of human-

Dolphins use sound to help them "see" underwater.

A whale swims near oil platforms.

made noise in waters around the United States. It also studies maps of animals' migration routes and favorite feeding spots. NOAA plans to combine all this information. This can help shipping and oil companies stay away from areas where ocean animals are most likely to be.

10   The International Maritime Organization is responsible for ocean safety worldwide. In 2014, it set guidelines to reduce the noise levels of commercial ships. Some ships now have quieter motors.

11   Scientists at NOAA plan to continue their research. They want to find clearer evidence of the effects of ocean noise pollution. This could lead to quieting down the world's oceans. Now, that's music to a whale's ears!

"Seeing" Down Deep

12   Dolphins are among the ocean animals that rely on echolocation. They use sound waves and echoes to locate objects. A dolphin sends sound waves through the water. Those sound waves bounce off an object and echo back to the dolphin.

13   The time it takes for the echo to reach the dolphin tells it how far away the object is. The way the sound echoes tells the dolphin the shape, size, and speed of the object.

14   Marine animals use echolocation for everything, from avoiding obstacles and predators to locating their next meal.

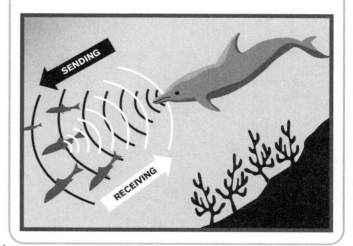

Name: _____

Directions: Read the article "Keep It Down!" Then answer the questions below.

1. Which of the following points did the author make in the article?

    A. Marine mammals don't have good hearing.

    B. The ocean has become too quiet in recent years.

    C. Humans cause noise pollution in the ocean.

    D. Ships should stop using propellers.

2. Which sentence from the article provides evidence that supports the answer to question 1?

    A. The deep ocean gets very little light. *(paragraph 3)*

    B. But that also means they could hear the sound of a ship or deep-sea oil drilling thousands of miles away. *(paragraph 5)*

    C. Icebergs screech as they grind against each other. *(paragraph 1)*

    D. Marine mammals also make sounds to communicate with one another. *(paragraph 4)*

3. According to scientists, which of the following is a possible effect of ocean noise pollution?

    A. The ocean's acoustics will become worse.

    B. Animals will change their migration routes.

    C. Some marine animals may have a tough time surviving.

    D. Whales will stop bellowing to one another.

4. Which statement best supports the answer to question 3?

    A. All that noise probably makes it harder for marine mammals to listen for predators. *(paragraph 8)*

    B. This could lead to quieting down the world's oceans. *(paragraph 11)*

    C. That means sound travels farther and faster through water than through air. *(paragraph 5)*

    D. So dolphins, porpoises, and many types of whales use sound to help them find their way around. *(paragraph 3)*

5. In paragraph 6, what sound is a ship using propellers compared to?

    A. A fish grunting

    B. The roar of a jet engine

    C. A whale bellowing

    D. The screech of moving icebergs

Name: _____

6. **If a place has good acoustics, it means that _____.**

   A. it sounds like you are underwater in it

   B. it can hold a lot of water

   C. you can hear sounds clearly in it

   D. it is very noisy

7. **Which detail provides evidence that people are working to lessen the amount of noise pollution in the ocean?**

   A. Some ships now have quieter motors. *(paragraph 10)*

   B. In addition, scientists have discovered that loud booms from ships can cause permanent injury. *(paragraph 8)*

   C. Studies have found that sea mammals are raising and changing their voices to be heard over all that noise. *(paragraph 6)*

   D. Scientists think all that racket is creating trouble for marine mammals. *(paragraph 2)*

8. **What is the purpose of the sidebar "'Seeing' Down Deep"? How does it support the main idea of the article? Use details from the sidebar and the article to support your answer.**

   _____

   _____

   _____

   _____

   _____

   _____

   _____

   _____

   _____

Keep It Down!

1   The ocean has never been a quiet place. Icebergs screech as they grind against each other. Whales bellow to one another over long distances. Some fish actually grunt to attract mates or ward off predators.

2   But now the world's waters are noisier than ever before. Deep-sea oil drilling, shipping, and other human activities are the reason. Scientists think all that racket is creating trouble for marine mammals that must be able to detect sounds to survive. Researchers are working to help find ways to turn down the ocean's volume.

"Seeing" With Sound

3   The deep ocean gets very little light. This makes it hard for marine mammals to use only their eyesight to get around. Dolphins, porpoises, and many types of whales use sound instead to help them "see." This is known as echolocation (see "'Seeing' Down Deep," next page).

4   Marine mammals also make sounds to communicate with one another. For example, some whales sing to attract mates. Dolphins call each other by whistles that serve as names.

5   The ocean has excellent **acoustics**. Sound travels farther and much faster through water than through air. That allows marine animals to communicate or find prey over long distances. Unfortunately, that also means they might hear the sound of a ship or deep-sea oil drilling thousands of miles away. Scientists are worried that the excessive noise is making it nearly impossible for the animals to find a quiet spot.

Can You Hear Me?

6   Ships that use propellers create the most ocean noise. These ships carry more than 90 percent of goods transported between countries. The booming noise they make can be louder than a jet engine. Studies have found that sea mammals are raising and altering their voices to be heard over all the underwater noise.

7   "For dolphins and whales, it's like trying to talk to a friend across a noisy classroom," says Jason Gedamke. He's a scientist at the National Oceanic and Atmospheric Administration (NOAA).

8   Scientists don't know exactly how having to "shout" is affecting marine animals. But they have discovered that loud booms from ships can cause permanent injury. Some animals have lost their hearing. And all that

Dolphins use sound to help them "see" underwater.

A whale swims near oil platforms.

human-made noise is likely making it harder for whales and dolphins to hunt, find mates, and listen for predators.

Lowering the Volume

9   What's being done to help these animals? For starters, NOAA has been mapping the noise levels of human activities in the waters around the United States. It plans to combine that data with maps that show animals' migration routes and favorite feeding spots. NOAA hopes shipping and oil companies will eventually use this information. This will help them avoid areas where ocean animals are most likely to be found.

10   Other steps are also being taken to make the ocean a quieter place. For example, some research ships, including NOAA's, are being built with quieter motors. In 2014, the International Maritime Organization set guidelines to reduce the noise levels of commercial ships. This group is responsible for ocean safety worldwide.

11   Scientists at NOAA say that's a major step in the right direction. They hope their research finds clearer evidence of the effects of ocean noise pollution. That could help bring about even more positive changes to quiet down the world's oceans. Now, that's music to a whale's ears!

"Seeing" Down Deep

12   Dolphins are among the ocean animals that rely on echolocation. They use sound waves and echoes to locate objects. A dolphin sends sound waves through the water. Those sound waves bounce off an object and echo back to the dolphin.

13   The time it takes for the echo to reach the dolphin tells it how far away the object is. The way the sound echoes tells the dolphin the shape, size, and speed of the object.

14   Marine animals use echolocation for everything, from avoiding obstacles and predators to locating their next meal.

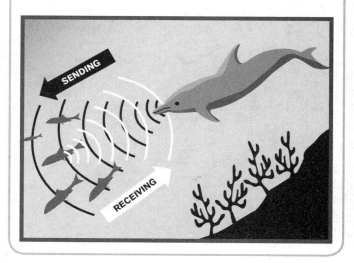

Name: _____

Directions: Read the article "Keep It Down!" Then answer the questions below.

1. Which of the following points did the author make in the article?

　　A. The ocean has become too quiet in recent years.

　　B. Humans cause noise pollution in the ocean.

　　C. Marine mammals don't have good hearing.

　　D. Ships should stop transporting goods internationally.

2. Which sentence from the article provides evidence that supports the answer to question 1?

　　A. Unfortunately, that also means they might hear the sound of a ship or deep-sea oil drilling thousands of miles away. *(paragraph 5)*

　　B. Marine mammals also make sounds to communicate with one another. *(paragraph 4)*

　　C. The deep ocean gets very little light. *(paragraph 3)*

　　D. Icebergs screech as they grind against each other. *(paragraph 1)*

3. According to scientists, which of the following is a possible effect of ocean noise pollution?

　　A. Whales will stop bellowing to one another.

　　B. Ships that use propellers will no longer be allowed to transport goods.

　　C. The ocean's acoustics will become worse.

　　D. Some marine animals may have a tough time surviving.

4. Which statement best supports the answer to question 3?

　　A. Ships that use propellers create the most ocean noise. *(paragraph 6)*

　　B. And all that human-made noise is likely making it harder for whales and dolphins to hunt, find mates, and listen for predators. *(paragraph 8)*

　　C. Dolphins, porpoises, and many types of whales use sound instead to help them "see." *(paragraph 3)*

　　D. Sound travels farther and much faster through water than through air. *(paragraph 5)*

5. In paragraph 6, what sound is the boom of a ship with propellers compared to?

　　A. The roar of a jet engine

　　B. A whale bellowing

　　C. The screech of moving icebergs

　　D. A fish grunting

Name: _____

6. If a place has good acoustics, it means that _____.

    A. it is very noisy

    B. you can hear sounds clearly in it

    C. it can hold a lot of water

    D. it sounds like you are underwater in it

7. Which detail provides evidence that people are working to lessen the amount of noise pollution in the ocean?

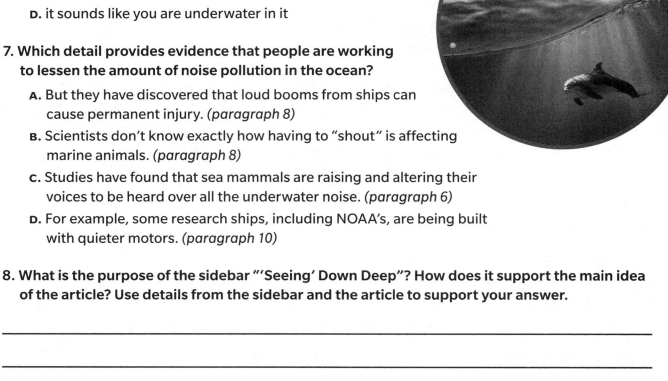

    A. But they have discovered that loud booms from ships can cause permanent injury. *(paragraph 8)*

    B. Scientists don't know exactly how having to "shout" is affecting marine animals. *(paragraph 8)*

    C. Studies have found that sea mammals are raising and altering their voices to be heard over all the underwater noise. *(paragraph 6)*

    D. For example, some research ships, including NOAA's, are being built with quieter motors. *(paragraph 10)*

8. What is the purpose of the sidebar "'Seeing' Down Deep"? How does it support the main idea of the article? Use details from the sidebar and the article to support your answer.

_____

_____

_____

_____

_____

_____

_____

_____

Scholastic News Leveled Informational Texts (Grade 5) © Scholastic Inc

Keep It Down!

1   The ocean has never been a quiet place. Icebergs screech as they grind against each other. Whales bellow to one another over long distances. Some fish actually grunt to attract mates or ward off predators.

2   But because of humans, the world's waters are now noisier than ever before. Deep-sea oil drilling, shipping, and other human activities are the reason. Scientists think all that racket is creating trouble for marine mammals that must be able to detect sounds to survive. Researchers are working to help find ways to turn down the ocean's volume.

"Seeing" With Sound

3   The deep ocean gets very little light, which makes it hard for marine mammals to rely only on their eyesight to get around. Dolphins, porpoises, and many types of whales use sound instead to help them "see." This is known as echolocation (see "'Seeing' Down Deep," next page).

4   Marine mammals also make sounds to communicate with one another. For example, some whales sing to attract mates, and dolphins call each other by whistles that serve as names.

5   The ocean has excellent **acoustics**. Sound travels farther and much faster through water than through air. That allows marine animals to communicate or find prey over long distances. Unfortunately, that also means they might hear the sound of a ship or deep-sea oil drilling thousands of miles away. Scientists are worried that the excessive noise is making it nearly impossible for the animals to find a quiet spot.

Can You Hear Me?

6   Ships that use propellers create the most ocean noise. These ships carry more than 90 percent of goods transported between countries. The booming noise they make can be louder than a jet engine. Studies have found that sea mammals are raising and altering their voices to be heard over all the underwater noise.

7   "For dolphins and whales, it's like trying to talk to a friend across a noisy classroom," says Jason Gedamke. He's a scientist at the National Oceanic and Atmospheric Administration (NOAA).

8   Scientists don't know exactly how having to "shout" is affecting marine animals.

Dolphins use sound to help them "see" underwater.

A whale swims near oil platforms.

But they have discovered that loud booms from ships can cause permanent injury. Some animals have lost their hearing. And all that human-made noise is likely making it harder for whales and dolphins to hunt, find mates, and listen for predators.

Lowering the Volume

9   What's being done to help these animals? For starters, NOAA has been mapping the noise levels of human activities in the waters around the United States. It plans to combine that data with maps that show animals' migration routes and favorite feeding spots. NOAA hopes shipping and oil companies will eventually use this information. This will help them avoid areas where ocean animals are most likely to be found.

10   Other steps are also being taken to make the ocean a quieter place. For example, some research ships, including NOAA's, are being built with quieter motors. In 2014, the International Maritime Organization set guidelines to reduce the noise levels of commercial ships. This group is responsible for ocean safety worldwide.

11   Scientists at NOAA say that's a major step in the right direction. They hope their research finds clearer evidence of the effects of ocean noise pollution. That could help bring about even more positive changes to quiet down the world's oceans. Now, that's music to a whale's ears!

"Seeing" Down Deep

12   Dolphins are among the ocean animals that rely on echolocation—the use of sound waves and echoes to locate objects. A dolphin sends sound waves through the water. Those sound waves bounce off an object and echo back to the dolphin.

13   The time it takes for the echo to reach the dolphin tells it how far away the object is. The way the sound echoes tells the dolphin the shape, size, and speed of the object.

14   Marine animals use echolocation for everything from avoiding obstacles and predators to locating their next meal.

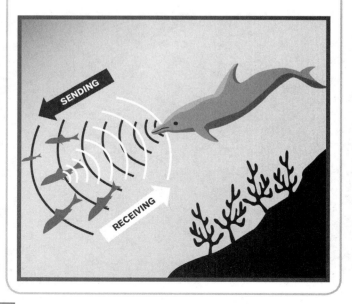

Scholastic News Leveled Informational Texts (Grade 5) © Scholastic Inc.

Name: _____

Directions: Read the article "Keep It Down!" Then answer the questions below.

1. Which of the following points did the author make in the article?

  A. Humans cause noise pollution in the ocean.

  B. The ocean has become too quiet in recent years.

  C. Marine mammals don't have good hearing.

  D. Ships should stop transporting goods internationally.

2. Which sentence from the article provides evidence that supports the answer to question 1?

  A. Marine mammals also make sounds to communicate with one another. *(paragraph 4)*

  B. Icebergs screech as they grind against each other. *(paragraph 1)*

  C. The deep ocean gets very little light, which makes it hard for marine animals to rely only on their eyesight to get around. *(paragraph 3)*

  D. Unfortunately, that also means they might hear the sound of a ship or deep-sea oil drilling thousands of miles away. *(paragraph 5)*

3. According to scientists, which of the following is a possible effect of ocean noise pollution?

  A. Ships that use propellers will no longer be allowed to transport goods.

  B. Some marine animals may have a tough time surviving.

  C. The ocean's acoustics will become worse.

  D. Whales will stop bellowing to one another.

4. Which statement best supports the answer to question 3?

  A. Ships that use propellers create the most ocean noise. *(paragraph 6)*

  B. Sound travels farther and much faster through water than through air. *(paragraph 5)*

  C. And all that human-made noise is likely making it harder for whales and dolphins to hunt, find mates, and listen for predators. *(paragraph 8)*

  D. Dolphins, porpoises, and many types of whales use sound instead to help them "see." *(paragraph 3)*

5. In paragraph 6, what sound is the boom of a ship using propellers compared to?

  A. A whale bellowing

  B. The screech of moving icebergs

  C. A fish grunting

  D. The roar of a jet engine

Name: _____

6. If a place has good acoustics, it means that _____.

    A. you can hear sounds clearly in it

    B. it can hold a lot of water

    C. it sounds like you are underwater in it

    D. it is very noisy

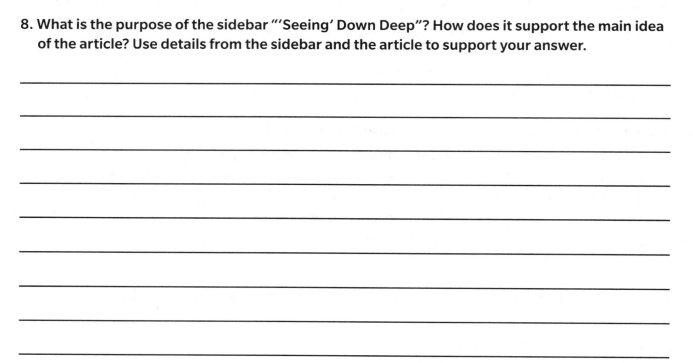

7. Which detail provides evidence that people are working to lessen the amount of noise pollution in the ocean?

    A. But they have discovered that loud booms from ships can cause permanent injury. *(paragraph 8)*

    B. Scientists don't know exactly how having to "shout" is affecting marine animals. *(paragraph 8)*

    C. For example, some research ships, including NOAA's, are being built with quieter motors. *(paragraph 10)*

    D. Studies have found that sea mammals are raising and altering their voices to be heard over all the underwater noise. *(paragraph 6)*

8. What is the purpose of the sidebar "'Seeing' Down Deep"? How does it support the main idea of the article? Use details from the sidebar and the article to support your answer.

_____

_____

_____

_____

_____

_____

_____

_____

Sunken City

1   Mummies and giant pyramids in the desert. That's what many people imagine when they think of Egypt. But some of the country's ancient treasures are buried underwater. Long ago, a city in Egypt fell into the sea. Now it lies on the ocean floor near Egypt's northern coast. In 2013, scientists brought up objects from this city to share with the world.

Clues to the Past

2   The city was known as Heracleion (hih-ra-KLEE-en). It sank about 1,200 years ago. Scientist Franck Goddio discovered the city in 2000. Since then, he and his team have been digging around it underwater. They've uncovered old gold coins, jewelry, giant statues, ships, and a sign. These **artifacts** have helped them learn about what life was like in Heracleion.

A statue from Heracleion

3   For example, people from other countries used to sail to Heracleion. They went to the city to trade goods, such as food and clothing.

4   "It was an important port for all ships coming into Egypt," says Goddio.

Secrets of the Deep

5   Goddio isn't sure how the city sank. He thinks an earthquake or a tidal wave may have caused it to fall into the sea.

6   "Stories from long ago tell of other cities in this area disappearing because of both of those things," explains Goddio.

7   But so far, the sinking of this city is still a mystery.

Site of Heracleion

Mediterranean Sea

ISRAEL

Alexandria

Cairo

EGYPT

LIBYA

Nile River

N W E S

Red Sea

U.S.

EGYPT

Africa

EQUATOR

SUDAN

Name: _____

Directions: Read the article "Sunken City." Then answer the questions below.

1. What is the article mostly about?

　A. The life of scientist Franck Goddio

　B. An ancient statue

　C. The sunken remains of an ancient city in Egypt

　D. An earthquake that destroyed ancient cities in Egypt

2. Which question can be answered by reading paragraph 1 of the article?

　A. What was life like in Heracleion?

　B. Why did Heracleion disappear?

　C. How did people from other parts of the world travel to Heracleion?

　D. Where in the ocean did scientists find Heracleion?

3. Which sentence from paragraph 1 best supports the answer to question 2?

　A. Long ago, a city in Egypt fell into the sea.

　B. Now it lies on the ocean floor near Egypt's northern coast.

　C. But some of the country's ancient treasures are buried underwater.

　D. In 2013, scientists brought up objects from this city to share with the world.

4. What does the word _artifacts_ mean as it is used in paragraph 2 of the article?

　A. Objects from long ago

　B. Clues in a mystery

　C. Stories

　D. People from faraway places

5. Which statement from the article best helps you understand the meaning of _artifacts_?

　A. It sank about 1,200 years ago. (_paragraph 2_)

　B. They've uncovered old gold coins, jewelry, giant statues, ships, and a sign. (_paragraph 2_)

　C. They went to the city to trade goods, such as food and clothing. (_paragraph 3_)

　D. Since then, he and his team have been digging around it underwater. (_paragraph 2_)

6. Which detail best supports the idea that Heracleion was an important port?

　A. Franck Goddio discovered Heracleion in 2000.

　B. No one knows for sure why Heracleion disappeared into the sea 1,200 years ago.

　C. People from other countries went to Heracleion to trade goods.

　D. Franck Goddio thinks Heracleion could have sunk because of an earthquake.

Name: _____

7. According to the article, which of the following happened first?

    A. Franck Goddio and his team discovered Heracleion.

    B. Franck Goddio and his team removed sand from artifacts.

    C. Scientists brought artifacts from the sunken city to the surface.

    D. Heracleion sank into the sea.

8. What is the purpose of the article's map?

    A. To show the location of Heracleion

    B. To show where different sunken cities around Egypt are located

    C. To show where earthquakes have struck Egypt in the past

    D. To show different routes people once took to get to Heracleion

9. What does Franck Goddio believe might have caused Heracleion to end up in the sea? Why does he believe this? Use details from the article to support your answer.

_____

_____

_____

_____

_____

_____

_____

Sunken City

1   Egypt is famous for its mummies and giant pyramids in the desert. But some of the country's ancient treasures are hidden underwater. Long ago, one of its cities fell into the sea. Now it lies on the ocean floor near Egypt's northern coast. In 2013, scientists lifted **artifacts** from that city to the surface to share with the world.

Clues to the Past

2   The city was known as Heracleion (hih-ra-KLEE-en). It sank into the sea 1,200 years ago. Scientist Franck Goddio discovered the city in 2000. Since then, he and his team have been removing layers of sand from what's left of it. They've uncovered objects such as old gold coins, jewelry, giant statues, ships, and a sign. These artifacts have helped scientists learn more what life was like in Heracleion.

A statue from Heracleion

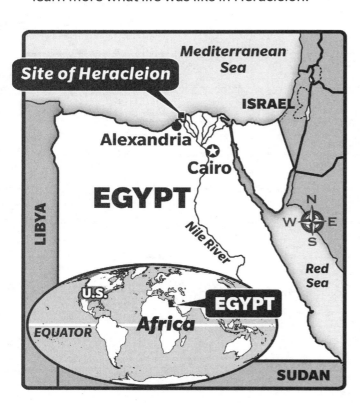

3   One thing that Goddio has learned is that people from other countries often sailed to Heracleion. They went to the city to trade goods, such as food and clothing, with the people who lived there.

4   "It was an important port for all ships coming into Egypt," says Goddio.

Secrets of the Deep

5   Goddio isn't sure how the city sank. He thinks that an earthquake or a tidal wave may have caused it to topple into the sea.

6   "Stories from long ago tell of other cities in this area disappearing because of both of those things," explains Goddio.

7   But so far, the sinking of this city remains a mystery.

Scholastic News Leveled Informational Texts (Grade 5) © Scholastic Inc.

Name: _____

Directions: Read the article "Sunken City." Then answer the questions below.

1. What is the article mostly about?

    A. An earthquake that destroyed ancient cities in Egypt

    B. The life of scientist Franck Goddio

    C. An ancient statue

    D. The sunken remains of an ancient city in Egypt

2. Which question can be answered by reading paragraph 1 of the article?

    A. Why did Heracleion disappear?

    B. Where in the ocean did scientists find Heracleion?

    C. What was life like in Heracleion?

    D. How did people from other parts of the world travel to Heracleion?

3. Which sentence from paragraph 1 best supports the answer to question 2?

    A. Now it lies on the ocean floor near Egypt's northern coast.

    B. Egypt is famous for its mummies and giant pyramids in the desert.

    C. In 2013, scientists lifted artifacts from that city to the surface to share with the world.

    D. But some of the country's ancient treasures are hidden underwater.

4. What does the word *artifacts* mean as it is used in paragraph 1 of the article?

    A. Clues in a mystery

    B. Stories

    C. Objects from long ago

    D. People from faraway places

5. Which statement from the article best helps you understand the meaning of *artifacts*?

    A. It sank into the sea 1,200 years ago. (*paragraph 2*)

    B. Since then, he and his team have been removing layers of sand from what's left of it. (*paragraph 2*)

    C. They went to the city to trade goods, such as food and clothing . . . (*paragraph 3*)

    D. They've uncovered objects such as old gold coins, jewelry, giant statues, ships, and a sign. (*paragraph 2*)

6. Which detail best supports the idea that Heracleion was an important port?

    A. Franck Goddio discovered Heracleion in 2000.

    B. People from other countries went to Heracleion to trade goods.

    C. No one knows for sure why Heracleion disappeared into the sea 1,200 years ago.

    D. Franck Goddio thinks Heracleion could have been sunk by an earthquake.

Name: _____

7. According to the article, which of the following happened first?

    A. Heracleion sank into the sea.

    B. Franck Goddio and his team discovered Heracleion.

    C. Franck Goddio and his team removed sand from artifacts.

    D. Scientists brought artifacts from the sunken city to the surface.

8. What is the purpose of the article's map?

    A. To show different routes people once took to get to Heracleion

    B. To show where earthquakes have struck Egypt in the past

    C. To show the location of Heracleion

    D. To show where different sunken cities around Egypt are located

9. What does Franck Goddio believe might have caused Heracleion to end up in the sea? Why does he believe this? Use details from the article to support your answer.

_____

_____

_____

_____

_____

_____

_____

_____

_____

Scholastic News Leveled Informational Texts (Grade 5) © Scholastic Inc.

Sunken City

1 Egypt is famous for its mummies and giant pyramids in the desert. But some of the country's ancient treasures are hidden underwater. A long-lost city lies on the ocean floor near Egypt's northern coast. In 2013, scientists lifted **artifacts** from that sunken city to the surface to share with the world.

Clues to the Past

2 The city, known as Heracleion (hih-ra-KLEE-en), disappeared beneath the waves 1,200 years ago. Scientist Franck Goddio discovered it in 2000. Since then, he and his team have been busy removing layers of sand from what's left of the city. They've uncovered objects such as old gold coins, jewelry, giant statues, ships, and a sign. These artifacts have helped scientists find out what life was once like in Heracleion.

A statue from Heracleion

3 One thing that Goddio has learned is that people from other countries often sailed to Heracleion. They went to the city to trade goods, such as food and clothing, with the people who lived there.

4 "It was an important port for all ships coming into Egypt," says Goddio.

Secrets of the Deep

5 Goddio isn't sure how the city sank. He thinks that an earthquake or a tidal wave may have caused it to topple into the sea.

6 "Stories from long ago tell of other cities in this area disappearing because of both of those things," explains Goddio.

7 But so far, the sinking of this city remains a mystery.

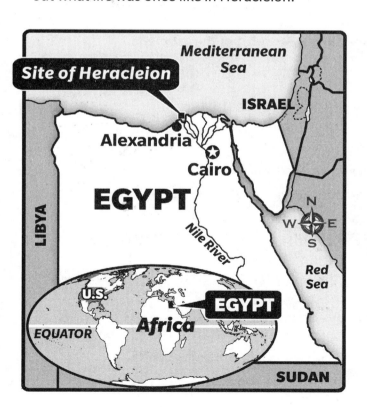

Site of Heracleion

Mediterranean Sea

ISRAEL

Alexandria

Cairo

EGYPT

Nile River

LIBYA

Red Sea

U.S.

Africa

EQUATOR

EGYPT

SUDAN

Name: _____

Directions: Read the article "Sunken City." Then answer the questions below.

1. What is the article mostly about?

   A. An ancient statue

   B. The sunken remains of an ancient city in Egypt

   C. An earthquake that destroyed ancient cities in Egypt

   D. The life of scientist Franck Goddio

2. Which question can be answered by reading paragraph 1 of the article?

   A. Where in the ocean did scientists find Heracleion?

   B. What was life like in Heracleion?

   C. Why did Heracleion disappear?

   D. How did people from other parts of the world travel to Heracleion?

3. Which sentence from paragraph 1 best supports the answer to question 2?

   A. Egypt is famous for its mummies and giant pyramids in the desert.

   B. But some of the country's ancient treasures are hidden underwater.

   C. A long-lost city lies on the ocean floor near Egypt's northern coast.

   D. In 2013, scientists lifted artifacts from that sunken city to the surface to share with the world.

4. What does the word *artifacts* mean as it is used in paragraph 1 of the article?

   A. Stories

   B. Clues in a mystery

   C. People from faraway places

   D. Objects from long ago

5. Which statement from the article best helps you understand the meaning of *artifacts*?

   A. The city, known as Heracleion, disappeared beneath the waves 1,200 years ago. *(paragraph 2)*

   B. Since then, he and his team have been busy removing layers of sand from what's left of it. *(paragraph 2)*

   C. They've uncovered objects such as old gold coins, jewelry, giant statues, ships, and a sign. *(paragraph 2)*

   D. They went to the city to trade goods, such as food and clothing . . . *(paragraph 3)*

6. Which detail best supports the idea that Heracleion was an important port?

   A. People from other countries went to Heracleion to trade goods.

   B. Franck Goddio discovered Heracleion in 2000.

   C. Franck Goddio thinks Heracleion could have been sunk by an earthquake.

   D. No one knows for sure why Heracleion disappeared into the sea 1,200 years ago.

7. According to the article, which of the following happened first?

   A. Franck Goddio and his team discovered Heracleion.

   B. Heracleion sank into the sea.

   C. Scientists brought artifacts from the sunken city to the surface.

   D. Franck Goddio and his team removed sand from artifacts.

8. What is the purpose of the article's map?

   A. To show where earthquakes have struck Egypt in the past

   B. To show different routes people once took to get to Heracleion

   C. To show where different sunken cities around Egypt are located

   D. To show the location of Heracleion

9. What does Franck Goddio believe might have caused Heracleion to end up in the sea? Why does he believe this? Use details from the article to support your answer.

_____

_____

_____

_____

_____

_____

_____

_____

The Ugly Truth

1 Which animal would you rather snuggle up with—a panda cub or a pig-nosed frog? Most people would say the panda. But not Lucy Cooke.

2 "I've always loved weird, freaky, and strange animals," she says.

3 Cooke is a scientist. She travels the globe to take photos and videos of the world's ugliest animals. She has also hosted TV specials to raise awareness about these creatures before it's too late. Many are endangered and could use a helping hand.

Animal Planet

4 There are more than 6,000 known endangered animal species in the world. These animals are in danger of dying out. You likely know that tigers, giant pandas, and some types of penguins are endangered. Animals like these get most of the attention from **conservation** groups. A study released in 2012 shows that this is no accident. The study found that animal-protection groups tend to focus on cute and cuddly creatures. That's because it's easy to convince people to help them.

Who Are You Calling Ugly?

5 Most endangered animals aren't adorable, however. Just look at the striped hyena, the proboscis monkey, or the blobfish (next page). Scientists say they need our help too. Every animal, no matter how it looks, plays an important role in an ecosystem.

6 Take frogs, for example. Sure, they're slimy. But Cooke explains that if they were to disappear from an ecosystem, the snakes and birds that feed on them could end up dying out too. At the same time, with no frogs to gobble them up, the number of mosquitoes and flies might grow out of control.

7 "We need to protect all of nature and not just the fluffy bits," Cooke says. "All animals have a job to do."

It's Not All About Looks

8 Cooke says there's a good reason some animals aren't cute and fuzzy. Often, the things we find unattractive in animals are adaptations. They help animals survive in the wild.

The pangolin's scales are made from the same material as our fingernails.

9   Take the pangolin, for example. This small mammal is Cooke's favorite endangered animal. It lives in Africa and Asia. Cooke calls it a "walking pinecone." Its body is covered with large, hard scales. But the pangolin's ugly body armor protects it from tigers and other predators.

10   Cooke teaches people about the importance of keeping pangolins and other ugly animals around. She wants people to appreciate all animals, no matter what they look like.

11   "Once you understand why they're ugly or odd," she says, "I hope you'll appreciate and want to save them as much as I do."

Creature Features

Striped Hyena

12   The state of the striped hyena is no laughing matter. Only about 10,000 of them still roam areas from North Africa to India. The hyena's front legs are much longer than its hind legs. So it appears to be limping when it walks. Striped hyenas are often killed by farmers who want to protect their crops and livestock.

Proboscis Monkey

13   Check out the honker on this guy! Proboscis monkeys have 4-inch-long noses that produce a loud sound. This attracts mates and scares off enemies. The monkeys' forest homes on the island of Borneo, in Southeast Asia, are being destroyed. And that's driving them toward extinction.

Blobfish

14   It's easy to see how this sea creature got its name. Blobfish live in the deep ocean near Australia. Their blobby bodies let them float just above the seafloor. These fish don't use a lot of energy chasing their next meal. Instead, they hover and wait to gobble up any prey that passes by. Unfortunately, blobfish often get caught in the nets of fishermen looking for crabs and lobsters.

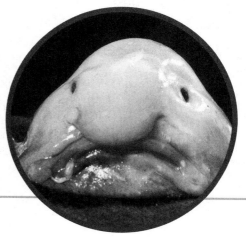

Name: _____

Directions: Read the article "The Ugly Truth." Then answer the questions below.

1. According to a study that came out in 2012, animal-protection groups _____.

    A. focus on cute creatures because most people like to help them

    B. focus on ugly animals because most people don't help them

    C. pay the most attention to cute animals because people like to buy them

    D. help both cute and ugly animals equally

2. Which phrase from paragraph 4 best helps you understand what the word *conservation* means?

    A. in danger of dying out

    B. endangered animal species

    C. get most of the attention

    D. animal-protection groups

3. What is the author's main point in the section "Who Are You Calling Ugly?"

    A. Many ugly creatures are endangered and need our help.

    B. All animals, even ugly ones, are important parts of an ecosystem.

    C. Pangolins have unique adaptations.

    D. Animal-protection groups are working to save giant pandas.

4. Which of the following does the author offer as evidence to support this point?

    A. A description of how the pangolin protects itself

    B. A study detailing the animals that conservation groups help

    C. An explanation of the effects of the disappearance of frogs on an ecosystem

    D. An explanation of the effects of the disappearance of snakes on an ecosystem

5. The pangolin's "ugly" adaptation is its _____.

    A. short hind legs

    B. 4-inch-long nose

    C. blobby body

    D. large, hard scales

6. Which detail from the article best explains the purpose of the pangolin's adaptation?

    A. protects it from tigers and other predators (*paragraph 9*)

    B. appears to be limping when it walks (*paragraph 12*)

    C. attracts mates and scares off enemies (*paragraph 13*)

    D. don't use a lot of energy chasing their next meal (*paragraph 14*)

7. **Which choice best describes Lucy Cooke's point of view about ugly animals?**

   A. She wants to save only strange-looking animals.

   B. She doesn't think they are very important.

   C. She thinks people should protect all animals, ugly ones included.

   D. She thinks we should focus on helping cute animals.

8. **According to the sidebar, what is the main reason proboscis monkeys are in danger of dying out?**

   A. They are being killed by farmers.

   B. Their forest habitat is being destroyed.

   C. Predators are wiping them out.

   D. They are being hunted too much.

9. **Write a letter to an animal-protection organization explaining why it should also focus on protecting ugly animals. Use at least two details from the text to support your points.**

_____

_____

_____

_____

_____

_____

_____

_____

The Ugly Truth

1. Which animal would you rather snuggle up with—a panda cub or the pig-nosed frog? Most people would say the panda, but not Lucy Cooke.

2. "I've always loved weird, freaky, and strange animals," she says.

3. Cooke is a scientist. She travels the globe to take photos and videos of the world's ugliest animals. She has also hosted TV specials to raise awareness about these creatures before it's too late. Many are endangered and could use a helping hand.

Animal Planet

4. There are more than 6,000 known endangered animal species in the world. These animals are in danger of dying out. You likely know that tigers, giant pandas, and some types of penguins are endangered. Animals like these get most of the attention from **conservation** groups. A study released in 2012 by Canadian scientist Ernie Small shows that this is no accident. He found that animal-protection groups tend to focus on cute and cuddly creatures. That's because it's easy to convince people to help them.

Who Are You Calling Ugly?

5. Most endangered animals aren't adorable, however. Just look at the striped hyena, the proboscis monkey, or the blobfish (next page). Scientists say they need our help too. Every animal, no matter how it looks, plays an important role in an ecosystem.

6. Take frogs, for example. Sure, they're slimy. But Cooke explains that if they were to disappear from an ecosystem, the snakes and birds that feed on them could end up dying out too. At the same time, with no frogs to gobble them up, the number of mosquitoes and flies might grow out of control.

7. "We need to protect all of nature and not just the fluffy bits," Cooke says. "All animals have a job to do."

It's Not All About Looks

8. Cooke says there's a good reason some animals aren't cute and fuzzy. Often, the things we find unattractive in animals are adaptations that help them survive in the wild.

9. She points to one of her favorite endangered animals as an example.

The pangolin's scales are made from the same material as our fingernails.

The pangolin is a small mammal that lives in Africa and Asia. Cooke calls it a "walking pinecone." Its body is covered from head to tail with large, hard scales. But the pangolin's ugly body armor protects it from tigers and other predators.

10   Cooke is working to educate people about the importance of keeping pangolins and other ugly animals around. She wants people to appreciate all animals, no matter what they look like.

11   "Once you understand why they're ugly or odd," she says, "I hope you'll appreciate and want to save them as much as I do."

Creature Features

Striped Hyena

12   The state of the striped hyena is no laughing matter. Only about 10,000 of them still roam areas from North Africa to India. The hyena's front legs are much longer than its hind legs, so it appears to be limping when it walks. Striped hyenas are often killed by farmers who want to protect their crops and livestock.

Proboscis Monkey

13   Check out the honker on this guy! Proboscis monkeys use their 4-inch-long noses to produce a loud sound that attracts mates and scares off enemies. The destruction of the monkeys' forest homes on the island of Borneo, in Southeast Asia, is driving them toward extinction.

Blobfish

14   It's easy to see how this sea creature got its name. Blobfish live in the deep ocean near Australia. Their blobby bodies let them float just above the seafloor, so they don't have to use a lot of energy chasing their next meal. Instead, they hover and wait to gobble up any prey that passes by. Unfortunately, blobfish often get caught in the nets of fishermen looking for crabs and lobsters.

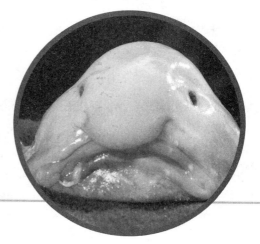

Name: _____

Directions: Read the article "The Ugly Truth." Then answer the questions below.

1. According to a study that came out in 2012, animal-protection groups _____.

   A. help both cute and ugly animals equally

   B. focus on cute creatures because most people like to help them

   C. focus on ugly animals because most people don't help them

   D. pay the most attention to cute animals because people like to buy them

2. **Which phrase from paragraph 4 best helps you understand what the word** *conservation* **means?**

   A. animal-protection groups

   B. get most of the attention

   C. endangered animal species

   D. in danger of dying out

3. What is the author's main point in the section "Who Are You Calling Ugly?"

   A. Animal-protection groups are working to save giant pandas.

   B. Many ugly creatures are endangered and need our help.

   C. Pangolins have unique adaptations.

   D. All animals, even ugly ones, are important parts of an ecosystem.

4. **Which of the following does the author offer as evidence to support this point?**

   A. A study detailing the animals that conservation groups help

   B. An explanation of the effects of the disappearance of frogs on an ecosystem

   C. A description of how the pangolin protects itself

   D. An explanation of the effects of the disappearance of snakes on an ecosystem

5. The pangolin's "ugly" adaptation is its _____.

   A. short hind legs

   B. large, hard scales

   C. blobby body

   D. 4-inch-long nose

6. **Which detail from the article best explains the purpose of the pangolin's adaptation?**

   A. attracts mates and scares off enemies *(paragraph 13)*

   B. don't have to use a lot of energy chasing their next meal *(paragraph 14)*

   C. protects it from tigers and other predators *(paragraph 9)*

   D. appears to be limping when it walks *(paragraph 12)*

Name: _____

7. Which choice best describes Lucy Cooke's point of view about ugly animals?

   A. She thinks people should protect all animals, ugly ones included.

   B. She wants to save only strange-looking animals.

   C. She thinks we should focus on helping cute animals.

   D. She doesn't think they are very important.

8. According to the sidebar, what is the main reason proboscis monkeys are in danger of dying out?

   A. They are being killed by farmers.

   B. Predators are wiping them out.

   C. They are being hunted too much.

   D. Their forest habitat is being destroyed.

9. Write a letter to an animal-protection organization explaining why it should also focus on protecting ugly animals. Use at least two details from the text to support your points.

   _____

   _____

   _____

   _____

   _____

   _____

   _____

   _____

The Ugly Truth

1   Which animal would you rather snuggle up with—a panda cub or the pig-nosed frog? Most people would say the panda, but not Lucy Cooke.

2   "I've always loved weird, freaky, and strange animals," she says.

3   Cooke is a scientist who travels the globe to take photos and videos of the world's ugliest animals. She has also hosted TV specials to raise awareness about these creatures before it's too late. Many are endangered and could use a helping hand.

Animal Planet

4   There are more than 6,000 known endangered animal species in the world. You likely know that tigers, giant pandas, and some types of penguins are among the animals in danger of dying out. Animals like these get most of the attention from **conservation** groups. A study released in 2012 by Canadian scientist Ernie Small shows that this is no accident. He found that animal-protection groups tend to focus on cute and cuddly creatures because it's easy to convince people to help them.

Who Are You Calling Ugly?

5   Most endangered animals aren't adorable, however. Just look at the striped hyena, the proboscis monkey, or the blobfish (next page). Scientists say they need our help too. Every animal, no matter how it looks, plays an important role in an ecosystem.

6   Take frogs, for example. Sure, they're slimy. But Cooke explains that if they were to disappear from an ecosystem, the snakes and birds that feed on them could end up dying out too. At the same time, with no frogs to gobble them up, the number of mosquitoes and flies might grow out of control.

7   "We need to protect all of nature and not just the fluffy bits," Cooke says. "All animals have a job to do."

It's Not All About Looks

8   Cooke says there's a good reason some animals aren't cute and fuzzy. Often, the things we find unattractive in animals are adaptations that help them survive in the wild.

9   She points to one of her favorite endangered animals, the pangolin,

The pangolin's scales are made from the same material as our fingernails.

as an example. The small mammal lives in Africa and Asia. Cooke calls it a "walking pinecone" because it's covered from head to tail with large, hard scales. But the pangolin's ugly body armor protects it from tigers and other predators.

10   Cooke is working to educate people about the importance of keeping pangolins and other ugly animals around. She wants people to appreciate all animals, no matter what they look like.

11   "Once you understand why they're ugly or odd," she says, "I hope you'll appreciate and want to save them as much as I do."

Creature Features

Striped Hyena

12   The state of the striped hyena is no laughing matter. Only about 10,000 of them still roam areas from North Africa to India. The hyena's front legs are much longer than its hind legs, so it appears to be limping when it walks. Striped hyenas are often killed by farmers who want to protect their crops and livestock.

Proboscis Monkey

13   Check out the honker on this guy! Proboscis monkeys use their 4-inch-long noses to produce a loud sound that attracts mates and scares off enemies. The destruction of the monkeys' forest homes on the island of Borneo, in Southeast Asia, is driving them toward extinction.

Blobfish

14   It's easy to see how this sea creature got its name. Blobfish live in the deep ocean near Australia. Their blobby bodies let them float just above the seafloor, so they don't have to use a lot of energy chasing their next meal. Instead, they hover and wait to gobble up any prey that passes by. Unfortunately, blobfish often get caught in the nets of fishermen looking for crabs and lobsters.

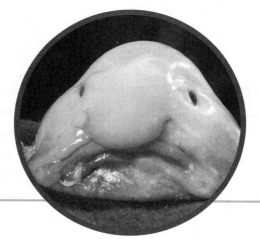

Name: _____

Directions: Read the article "The Ugly Truth." Then answer the questions below.

1. **According to a study that came out in 2012, animal-protection groups _____.**

    A. pay the most attention to cute animals because people like to buy them

    B. focus on ugly animals because most people don't help them

    c. help both cute and ugly animals equally

    D. focus on cute creatures because most people like to help them

2. **Which phrase from paragraph 4 best helps you understand what the word** *conservation* **means?**

    A. endangered animal species

    B. animal-protection groups

    c. get most of the attention

    D. in danger of dying out

3. **What is the author's main point in the section "Who Are You Calling Ugly?"**

    A. Many ugly creatures are endangered and need our help.

    B. Animal-protection groups are working to save giant pandas.

    c. All animals, even ugly ones, are important parts of an ecosystem.

    D. Pangolins have unique adaptations.

4. **Which of the following does the author offer as evidence to support this point?**

    A. An explanation of the effects of the disappearance of frogs on an ecosystem

    B. A description of how the pangolin protects itself

    c. A study detailing the animals that conservation groups help

    D. An explanation of the effects of the disappearance of snakes on an ecosystem

5. **The pangolin's "ugly" adaptation is its _____.**

    A. large, hard scales

    B. short hind legs

    c. 4-inch-long nose

    D. blobby body

6. **Which detail from the article best explains the purpose of the pangolin's adaptation?**

    A. don't have to use a lot of energy chasing their next meal (*paragraph 14*)

    B. protects it from tigers and other predators (*paragraph 9*)

    c. attracts mates and scares off enemies (*paragraph 13*)

    D. appears to be limping when it walks (*paragraph 12*)

7. Which choice best describes Lucy Cooke's point of view about ugly animals?

    A. She doesn't think they are very important.

    B. She wants to save only strange-looking animals.

    c. She thinks we should focus on helping cute animals.

    D. She thinks people should protect all animals, ugly ones included.

8. According to the sidebar, what is the main reason proboscis monkeys are in danger of dying out?

    A. They are being killed by farmers.

    B. Predators are wiping them out.

    c. Their forest habitat is being destroyed.

    D. They are being hunted too much.

9. Write a letter to an animal-protection organization explaining why it should also focus on protecting ugly animals. Use at least two details from the text to support your points.

_____

_____

_____

_____

_____

_____

_____

_____

_____

Answer Key

A CHAMPION FOR CHIMPS

page 7
1. c **2.** Answers will vary. Sample response: *Goodall became interested in chimps after reading* Tarzan of the Apes *as a kid. As an adult, she met scientist Louis Leakey, who sent her to study chimps in Africa.*
3. Answers will vary. Sample response: *To study or watch something carefully to learn more about it*
4. Answers will vary. Sample response: *Humans destroy forests where chimps live, hunt chimps for food and to be sold, put them in commercials, and keep them as pets.* **5.** Answers will vary. Sample response: *Like humans, chimps use tools and form family bonds.*

page 9
1. b **2.** Answers will vary. Sample response: *Goodall became interested in chimps after reading Tarzan of the Apes as a kid. As an adult, she met scientist Louis Leakey, who sent her to study chimps in Africa.* **3.** Answers will vary. Sample response: *To study or watch something carefully to learn more about it* **4.** Answers will vary. Sample response: *Like humans, chimps use tools and form family bonds.*
5. Answers will vary. Sample response: *Humans destroy forests where chimps live, hunt chimps for food and to be sold, put them in commercials, and keep them as pets.*

page 11
1. Answers will vary. Sample response: *Goodall became interested in chimps after reading Tarzan of the Apes as a kid. As an adult, she met scientist Louis Leakey, who sent her to study chimps in Africa.*
2. Answers will vary. Sample response: *To study or watch something carefully to learn more about it*
3. d **4.** Answers will vary. Sample response: *Humans destroy forests where chimps live, hunt chimps for food and to be sold, put them in commercials, and keep them as pets.* **5.** Answers will vary. Sample response: *Like humans, chimps use tools and form family bonds.*

IF YOU CAN'T BEAT 'EM, EAT 'EM!

page 13
1. c **2.** d **3.** a **4.** a **5.** d **6.** Answers will vary. Sample response: *In the article "If You Can't Beat 'Em, Eat 'Em!" experts say the solution to the lionfish problem may be people, the world's top predator. The article explains, "Lionfish have no natural predators in these waters. So they quickly multiplied." Experts think humans need to step in and help control the lionfish population. The author most likely ended the article with this point to emphasize that the best, and possibly only, solution to the problem presented in the article is that people help cut down the lionfish population.*

page 16
1. b **2.** c **3.** d **4.** b **5.** a **6.** Answers will vary. Sample response: *In the article "If You Can't Beat 'Em, Eat 'Em!" experts say the solution to the lionfish problem lies with people, the world's top predator. The article explains, "With no natural predators in these waters, the lionfish quickly multiplied." So people need to step in and help control the population of these fish, since no other predator exists naturally in Florida's waters. The author most likely ended the article with this point to emphasize that the best, and possibly only, solution to the problem presented in the article is that people help combat the lionfish population.*

page 19
1. d **2.** a **3.** b **4.** d **5.** c **6.** Answers will vary. Sample response: *In the article "If You Can't Beat 'Em, Eat 'Em!" experts say the solution to the lionfish problem lies with humans, the world's top predator. The article explains, "With no natural predators in these waters, the lionfish quickly multiplied." So people need to step in and help control the population of these fish since no other predator exists naturally in Florida's waters. The author most likely ended the article with this point to emphasize that the best, and possibly only, solution to the problem presented in the article is that people help combat the lionfish population.*

WALKING THE AMAZON

page 22
1. c **2.** b **3.** a and d **4.** c **5.** b **6.** Answers will vary. Sample response: *Ed Stafford's adventure was challenging because he faced dangerous animals along the way, including snakes, crocodiles, and electric eels. Another challenge was crossing through tribal land. In Peru, he was threatened by the chief of a native tribe.*

page 24
1. a **2.** c **3.** b and f **4.** b **5.** a **6.** Answers will vary. Sample response: *Ed Stafford's adventure was*

challenging because he faced dangerous animals along the way, including snakes, crocodiles, and electric eels. Another challenge was crossing through tribal land. In Peru, he was threatened by the chief of a native tribe.

page 26

1. d **2.** a **3.** c and e **4.** a **5.** d **6.** Answers will vary. Sample response: *Ed Stafford's adventure was challenging because he faced dangerous animals along the way, including snakes, crocodiles, and electric eels. Another challenge was crossing through tribal land. In Peru, he was threatened by the chief of a native tribe.*

INVASION OF THE DRONES

page 29

1. b **2.** a **3.** d **4.** b **5.** c **6.** Answers will vary. Sample response: *Professor Hillary Farber thinks there needs to be a "balance" when it comes to using drones. People should be able to use drones in a safe way that doesn't invade other people's privacy. I think the FAA is trying to find that balance by creating rules for the use of drones. It also created a national drone registry. People now have to register their drones when they buy them. This will help officials find the owner of a drone that flies where it shouldn't.*

page 32

1. c **2.** d **3.** a **4.** a **5.** b **6.** Answers will vary. Sample response: *Professor Hillary Farber thinks there needs to be a "balance" when it comes to using drones. People should be able to use drones in a safe way that doesn't invade other people's privacy. I think the FAA is trying to find that balance by creating rules for the use of drones. It also created a national drone registry. People now have to register their drones when they buy them. This will help officials find the owner of a drone that flies where it shouldn't.*

page 35

1. d **2.** c **3.** c **4.** d **5.** a **6.** Answers will vary. Sample response: *Professor Hillary Farber thinks there needs to be a "balance" when it comes to using drones. People should be able to use drones in a safe way that doesn't invade other people's privacy. I think the FAA is trying to find that balance by creating rules for the use of drones. It also created a national drone registry. People now have to register their drones when they buy them. This will help officials find the owner of a drone that flies where it shouldn't.*

A BATTLE OVER BAGS

page 37

1. a **2.** c **3.** c **4.** b **5.** d **6.** b **7.** Opinions will vary.

page 40

1. b **2.** d **3.** a **4.** d **5.** a **6.** c **7.** Opinions will vary.

page 43

1. d **2.** b **3.** b **4.** c **5.** c **6.** d **7.** Opinions will vary.

KEEP IT DOWN!

page 47

1. c **2.** b **3.** c **4.** a **5.** b **6.** c **7.** a **8.** Answers will vary. Sample response: *The purpose of the sidebar is to describe how dolphins use sound waves and echoes to survive in the ocean. It gives examples of how dolphins rely on echolocation to find food and avoid predators. For example, the text states, "The way the sound echoes tells the dolphin the shape, size, and speed of the object." This sidebar supports the main idea of the article because it shows how important sound is in the daily lives of dolphins. If the noise-pollution problem created by deep-sea oil drilling and shipping is not fixed, marine animals like dolphins will have trouble using echolocation. They may not be able to survive in the ocean as well as they once did.*

page 51

1. b **2.** a **3.** d **4.** b **5.** a **6.** b **7.** d **8.** Answers will vary. Sample response: *The purpose of the sidebar is to describe how dolphins use sound waves and echoes to survive in the ocean. It gives examples of how dolphins rely on echolocation to find food and avoid predators. For example, the text states, "The way the sound echoes tells the dolphin the shape, size, and speed of the object." This sidebar supports the main idea of the article because it shows how important sound is in the daily lives of dolphins. If the noise-pollution problem created by deep-sea oil drilling and shipping is not fixed, marine animals like dolphins will have trouble using echolocation. They may not be able to survive in the ocean as well as they once did.*

page 55

1. a **2.** d **3.** b **4.** c **5.** d **6.** a **7.** c **8.** Answers will vary. Sample response: *The purpose of the sidebar is to describe how dolphins use sound waves and echoes to survive in the ocean. It gives examples of how dolphins rely on echolocation to find food and* avoid predators. For example, the text states, "The way the sound echoes tells the dolphin the shape, size, and speed of the object." This sidebar supports the main idea of the article because it shows how important sound is in the daily lives of dolphins. If the noise-pollution problem created by deep-sea oil drilling and shipping is not fixed, marine animals like dolphins will have trouble using echolocation. They may not be able to survive in the ocean as well as they once did.

SUNKEN CITY

page 58
1. c **2.** d **3.** b **4.** a **5.** b **6.** c **7.** d **8.** a
9. Answers will vary. Sample response: *Franck Goddio does not know for certain why Heracleion sank into the sea, but he believes that an earthquake or a tidal wave could have been to blame. The reason for this belief is that stories from long ago describe other cities in this area disappearing because of those natural disasters.*

page 61
1. d **2.** b **3.** a **4.** c **5.** d **6.** b **7.** a **8.** c
9. Answers will vary. Sample response: *Franck Goddio does not know for certain why Heracleion sank into the sea, but he believes that an earthquake or a tidal wave could have been to blame. The reason for this belief is that stories from long ago describe other cities in this area disappearing because of those natural disasters.*

page 64
1. b **2.** a **3.** c **4.** d **5.** c **6.** a **7.** b **8.** d
9. Answers will vary. Sample response: *Franck Goddio does not know for certain why Heracleion sank into the sea, but he believes that an earthquake or a tidal wave could have been to blame. The reason for this belief is that stories from long ago describe other cities in this area disappearing because of those natural disasters.*

THE UGLY TRUTH

page 68
1. a **2.** d **3.** b **4.** c **5.** d **6.** a **7.** c **8.** b
9. Answers will vary. Sample response: *Dear [animal-protection organization]: It's wonderful that you're working to protect endangered animals, but you should focus on protecting ugly animals too, not just cute and cuddly ones. No matter what it looks like, every animal plays an important role in an ecosystem. For example, frogs may be slimy, but if they disappeared from an ecosystem, the animals that feed on them, such as snakes and birds, could end up dying too. And the population of bugs that frogs feed on could grow out of control. Also, often, the features we find unattractive are actually adaptations that help animals survive. For example, a proboscis monkey's long nose produces a sound that attracts mates and scares off enemies.*

page 72
1. b **2.** a **3.** d **4.** b **5.** b **6.** c **7.** a **8.** d
9. Answers will vary. Sample response: *Dear [animal-protection organization]: It's wonderful that you're working to protect endangered animals, but you should focus on protecting ugly animals too, not just cute and cuddly ones. No matter what it looks like, every animal plays an important role in an ecosystem. For example, frogs may be slimy, but if they disappeared from an ecosystem, the animals that feed on them, such as snakes and birds, could end up dying too. And the population of bugs that frogs feed on could grow out of control. Also, often, the features we find unattractive are actually adaptations that help animals survive. For example, a proboscis monkey's long nose produces a sound that attracts mates and scares off enemies.*

page 76
1. d **2.** b **3.** c **4.** a **5.** a **6.** b **7.** d **8.** c
9. Answers will vary. Sample response: *Dear [animal-protection organization]: It's wonderful that you're working to protect endangered animals, but you should focus on protecting ugly animals too, not just cute and cuddly ones. No matter what it looks like, every animal plays an important role in an ecosystem. For example, frogs may be slimy, but if they disappeared from an ecosystem, the animals that feed on them, such as snakes and birds, could end up dying too. And the population of bugs that frogs feed on could grow out of control. Also, often, the features we find unattractive are actually adaptations that help animals survive. For example, a proboscis monkey's long nose produces a sound that attracts mates and scares off enemies.*